Praise for *High-Performance Pay*

"Effective leadership requires making rewards count. *High-Performance Pay* is a leader's primer on how to recognize and reward excellence—a key ingredient of organizational success."

—**James O'Toole**, research professor, Center for Effective Organizations, University of Southern California, author of *Creating the Good Life* and co-author of *The New American Workplace*

"I always look for the applicability of pay concepts to a global workforce. Pat and Jay present a pay philosophy and related concepts that apply to any company or organization that seeks to achieve superior business performance wherever they operate in the world."

—**D. Thomas Dale**, vice president, human resources, Pulse Inc., a Technitrol company

"With thoughtful insight, *High-Performance Pay* gets to the heart of what it takes to truly get what we pay for to make our organizations great. In doing so, Pat and Jay build on their early work in *The New Pay* and *Pay People Right!*, by offering win-win strategies that connect the sound ideals of total rewards—*individual growth, compelling future, positive workplace* and *total pay*—with high performance. A great 'next generation' read for leaders who want to create a workplace brand that attracts the right people to do the right things."

—**Mark A. Speare**, senior associate director for patient affairs, human resources and marketing, UCLA Heath System

"*High-Performance Pay* is not for a bookshelf. It should be marked up, dog-eared and well worn by successful readers. This is an action book. Put Zingheim and Schuster's wisdom in action. Your employees and customers will thank you for doing so."

—**Dennis Campos**, human resources director, Los Angeles Biomedical Research Institute and adjunct professor, Claremont Graduate University

"The mark of today's successful compensation and human resources professionals is their ability to partner with their business leaders to drive a level of performance that enables the meeting and exceeding of business goals. Pat and Jay have again given us the go-to book for developing strategies and tactics for driving that peak level of performance in our organizations given today's challenging business environment."

—**Leslie M. Stevens, CCP, CEBS**, director compensation, Starbucks Coffee Co. and WorldatWork board member and faculty

"Having spent my entire career in the compensation and benefits field, this work represents the most up-to-date compendium of 'must know' compensation solutions I have seen in one book. I hope Pat and Jay are willing to update this book five years from now."

—**Randolph Wm. Keuch**, vice president, total rewards, HJ Heinz Co.

"Pat Zingheim and Jay Schuster show that pay systems must treat investments in total rewards like the vital business decisions they are, incorporating talent segmentation, logical decision principles and agility."

—**Dr. John W. Boudreau**, research director, Center for Effective Organizations and professor, management and organization, Marshall School of Business, University of Southern California and co-author of *Beyond HR: The New Science of Human Capital*

"In an era of heightened governance and increased transparency, linking pay and performance is more critical than ever. All stakeholders demand high performance. In *High-Performance Pay*, Zingheim and Schuster show how to create a sustainable high-performing culture, and more importantly, how to keep it on course as business needs change."

—**Laura Thanasse**, vice president compensation strategy, Sun Life Financial Inc.

"Zingheim and Schuster continue to push the envelope in providing practical strategies that will truly move the needle in the effectiveness of your company's compensation program. A must read for anyone desiring to get the most out of the reward budget in an ever-increasing dynamic business environment!"

—**Kerry Chou**, director, global compensation and benefits, ON Semiconductor

"In their previous book *Pay People Right!*, Zingheim and Schuster highlighted the need to focus on total rewards when developing an effective employment value proposition. *High-Performance Pay* takes this concept forward and challenges the reader to apply it in ways that will drive successful business performance. This new book provides a window into the future of compensation strategy along with some practical advice and case studies. An essential guide for all compensation professionals."

—**Irene Kohut**, director, global compensation, Nortel

"A comprehensive and thought-provoking book about the evolution of change for a compensation/benefits professional to a total rewards professional. Reading this book emphasized the importance of linking pay and rewards to business goals, providing pragmatic examples of how a total rewards professional can be an agent of change for creating and sustaining high-performing organizations."

—**Karen F. Ickes**, senior vice president, total rewards, Wendy's International Inc.

"Pat Zingheim and Jay Schuster once again demonstrate why they are the thought-leaders in compensation design. Benefit by the broad arc of strategic compensation ideas found in *High-Performance Pay*."

—**David J. Cichelli**, senior vice president, The Alexander Group Inc.
and author of *Compensating the Sales Force*

HIGH-
Performance
PAY

FAST FORWARD TO BUSINESS SUCCESS

Patricia K. Zingheim
Jay R. Schuster

About WorldatWork®

WorldatWork (www.worldatwork.org) is the association for human resources professionals focused on attracting, motivating and retaining employees. Founded in 1955, WorldatWork provides practitioners with knowledge leadership to effectively implement total rewards— compensation, benefits, work-life, performance and recognition, development and career opportunities—by connecting employee engagement to business performance. WorldatWork supports its 30,000 members and customers in 30 countries with thought leadership, education, publications, research and certification.

The WorldatWork group of registered marks includes: WorldatWork®, workspan®, Certified Compensation Professional or CCP®, Certified Benefits Professional® or CBP, Global Remuneration Professional or GRP®, Work-Life Certified Professional or WLCP™, WorldatWork Society of Certified Professionals®, and Alliance for Work-Life Progress® or AWLP®.

WorldatWork.
The Total Rewards Association™

WorldatWork Press
www.worldatwork.org

To Bebe Brenda Beebers

Table of Contents

Foreword

At many companies—and in many industries—total rewards systems are in trouble. They were built upon a series of premises that no longer hold true. The world of work is rapidly changing, but the designs of pay, benefit and total rewards systems are stuck in the mud.

A primary challenge for all leaders is sustaining or enhancing business results. To add value to the business, rewards must be part of the business solution. Today that is often not the case. Only when businesses achieve goals and attract the best people with the top skill and talent that can be translated into real performance can all the elements of total rewards be retained. So the key issue is making pay for performance real—many talk about this but it has not yet become prevailing practice. Companies need to either find ways to improve performance and relate increasing total rewards costs to results or change what they offer.

Think about other major problems that exist. It is hard to open a newspaper and not find an article about company benefit plans. Health-care costs have increased so dramatically that for many companies it is the fastest-rising expense on the income statement, rising in many cases more quickly than sales or profits. This is leading companies to change how they approach health care. Almost all employees are feeling the pinch of higher premiums, larger deductibles and bigger co-pays or coinsurance payments. Consumer-driven health plans are increasing in number as companies hope that an ounce of health-care consumerism will yield a pound of reduced health-care expense.

Retirement plans are also under fire. Companies are discovering they can no longer afford their traditional defined benefit pension plans. In some industries—automobile manufacturers, airlines and steel producers—these obligations threaten the financial viability of many large employers. As these plans are closed to new entrants or frozen for existing employees, they are being replaced with smaller, but more affordable, retirement and/or savings plans.

Stock plans are also in a state of stress. U.S. accounting rules have recently changed to require expensing of stock option grants on company financial statements. Prior to this accounting change, virtually every publicly traded company offered stock options to its executives and other senior employees. At some companies, all employees periodically received stock options. With the accounting change, U.S. companies took a fresh look at their stock granting practices and most changed something. Some employees, the most unlucky, simply stopped receiving grants. Others still received stock grants but they were smaller. In other cases, the nature of the stock grant changed from stock options to restricted stock or some form of performance-based long-term incentive.

On top of this rapid change, we have discovered a surprising number of companies were quietly backdating their stock option grants, to pretend that they were granted on an earlier date at a more favorable strike price. It is still too early to tell what the ramifications of this unfortunate practice will be on total rewards systems going forward.

The truth is, the entire total rewards framework that emerged in the 1980s and 1990s is simply unsustainable. As Thomas Friedman points out in *The World Is Flat*, the world is rapidly globalizing whether we like it or not. The economics of doing business are changing forever, and we can either change too or get left behind. Shareholders, who for decades were very silent, can now be heard with a roar. They have a lot to say about how executives and employees are compensated and how the company makes use of stock in compensation and benefits arrangements. Congress, the SEC and the IRS have also been paying attention to the various corporate scandals of recent years and have introduced new legislation, rules and regulations impacting what companies can or cannot do in pay and benefits systems.

Lastly, the workplace is getting more complicated. Most companies have employees from four generations in the same workplace. Recent generational diversity studies have shown that these generational groups are not homogeneous. What they expect to put into work and what they expect to receive in exchange are not the same. The "good ole" cookie-cutter approach to total rewards leaves many of these folks dissatisfied, some unmotivated. This is not a prescription for success in an increasingly competitive world.

The good news is this situation is entirely fixable. Most total rewards systems do not have to be scrapped, they have simply become ineffective. Using an automobile metaphor, they are in need of a major tune-up. This tune-up needs to reflect the new realities of work now and in the future. It needs to reflect what is in the hearts and minds of current and future workers. It needs to reflect the changing expectations of relevant external constituents. In short, it needs fresh thinking.

Pat Zingheim and Jay Schuster are fresh thinkers. They have shown in their two previous books, *The New Pay* and *Pay People Right!*, that they are not afraid to challenge the status quo. Not only do they paint a picture of what is wrong, but they also offer a thoughtful analysis of the situation, and actionable ideas and solutions to improve the situation. Pat and Jay were among the first to speak out on behalf of total rewards and were early in presenting the field with a total rewards framework that went well beyond traditional compensation and benefits. Their work caused many companies to rethink their approach to compensation and benefits, into a more holistic total rewards mindset. WorldatWork awarded Pat and Jay its highest honor, the Keystone Award, for their pioneering work in transforming practitioner thinking from siloed compensation and benefits to integrated total rewards.

Pat and Jay are not ones to rest on their laurels. They once again sensed something was amiss, and they penned this new text, *High-Performance Pay: Fast Forward to Business Success*, in response. They believe total rewards systems play a unique and important role in creating high-performance organizations. However, they see many companies' total rewards practices are stuck following conventional wisdom, often leading to less-than-high-performance pay solutions. They further believe that many of these solutions are no longer economically viable and lead to many of the gut-wrenching downsizing, outsourcing and offshoring actions that have come in the face of a business or industry downturn. They have presented 18 chapters of ideas about how to remake a total rewards system into a high-performance system, how to properly link the total rewards system to the operational side of the business to drive results, and how to create "win-win" solutions for companies and their employees.

As usual, their ideas are thought provoking and insightful. Their solutions are clear and actionable. Once again, Pat and Jay have their fingers on the pulse of change.

Michael Davis
Vice President, General Mills
Chairman of the Board, WorldatWork
October 2006

Preface and Acknowledgements

High-Performance Pay: Fast Forward to Business Success is about why and how to pay for performance—really do it and not just talk about it. Our book suggests how businesses can best develop pay initiatives that help create a healthy, exciting, and positive performance culture where success is shared and pay is based on performance.

We believe nearly every leader and employee want to do the right thing. Pay is only one element in making work attractive, however, few will work unless they are paid. So pay represents one potentially major link between people and their employer. We wrote this book to help business leaders close the knowing-doing gap as it relates to paying for performance—it is time to put real meaning into how pay is designed and managed throughout the world.

We appreciate our clients and other friends who have helped us formulate our beliefs about pay and total rewards by letting us continuously learn from them about what matters and how people add value.

We are grateful to Michael Davis for writing the foreword because he has added a valuable perspective to the book.

Our appreciation also extends to Marvin Dertien, David J. Thomsen and Paul Weatherhead. Without their contributions, chapters 8, 14 and 15, respectively, would not have been possible.

We want to thank WorldatWork for publishing this book and Dan Cafaro for suggesting it. We deeply appreciate WorldatWork's board of directors giving us the 2006 Keystone Award. Being recognized by our colleagues is a great honor, particularly because WorldatWork provides such high-quality content and services to its members.

We also want to thank Delene Smith, who has worked with us for more than 21 years, for her contributions over the years and helping us to bring this book to completion.

We dedicate this book to our cat Bebe because she brings joy and teaches her own meaningful lessons in living.

Patricia K. Zingheim and Jay R. Schuster

Los Angeles, Calif., January 2007

Introduction

High-Performance Pay: Fast Forward to Business Success celebrates leaders who not only view pay as a powerful tool to help drive business and employee success but also truly pay for performance. This book is about how pay can meaningfully help to create a performance culture and a high-performance organization. People and businesses thrive when they are successful so we do not believe leaders have any other reasonable choice than paying for performance. We believe paying for results, skill and competence is just good common sense—if you do not pay for these important business and talent priorities, what should you pay for?

The objective is improved business results so all stakeholders win—employees, customers, leaders, owners and the community. Pay has always focused principally on competitiveness. But with automation and compensation information on the Internet, the opportunity exists to reward beyond just competitiveness—to decipher what people want and how they value what they want as well as discover how to communicate and reward more effectively what the business wants to accomplish.

Any changes made to pay programs get everyone's attention. People listen to the messages that pay delivers so leaders must determine and communicate clearly the linkages. We believe it is impossible to create an atmosphere of high performance if results are not strongly rewarded.

The mission for pay has not changed over the years. It is still creating a win-win for businesses and people, but the definition of win changes over time for each party and the tools to achieve the win-win have improved. Business and total rewards leaders are in the driver's seat creating that value proposition. They must understand what the enterprise needs to accomplish—both in results and how it wants to operate (its values)—and proactively set the course with programs and do it with integrity. At the same time, pay and other rewards must engage people and be customized to the organization's message and metrics and what people value. Because total pay is a major opportunity and cost for the organization, this means exciting times ahead.

Basis for *High-Performance Pay: Fast Forward to Business Success*

Our book, *The New Pay*, was published in 1992 and now more organizations are using variable pay and incentives. Variable pay has extended more broadly below management and incentive opportunities have increased. These important changes have resulted in stronger engagement of employees as stakeholders in the organization's future and the creation of a win-win relationship between workforces and their organizations. Since 2000 when we published our book *Pay People Right!*, organizations have increasingly focused on total rewards that, depending on the definition, include total pay, individual growth, compelling future and positive workplace.

High-Performance Pay: Fast Forward to Business Success focuses on what has occurred since then. Innovation continues in the pay and rewards field. In no other area of HR have positive gains been more dramatic. And we predict that the total rewards field will continue to grow, become increasingly more challenging, and experience a surge of new ideas and practical applications that will magnify successful performance of organizations and help create performance cultures.

Clarifying Your Total Rewards Belief System

Over the years, we have developed and refined our beliefs about what creates a high-performance organization and provide this framework as an introduction to this book. We believe business leaders who are responsible for total rewards must develop and articulate their own sets of beliefs so they can facilitate high performance in organizations. The goal for HR professionals is to advise and educate leadership about decisions that favor performance over alternatives to performance. Their role is to help close the gap between knowing and doing. Although many know what should be done, the objective is to encourage many more people to act on what is the right thing to do and stay the course once they start. Here we are suggesting you think about your total rewards beliefs, and we give a jump start to refine and clarify your thinking, regardless of your beliefs.

Exhibit 1 provides examples of building a total rewards belief system to facilitate high performance by contrasting some beliefs for the total pay component of total rewards and for two areas—reward customization and fairness—that apply to all four components of total rewards (total pay, individual growth, compelling future and positive workplace).

In Exhibit 2, alternative possible total rewards beliefs continue in the areas of goal setting, performance management, managing superkeepers and managing out people who are either poor fits for the organization or poor performers.

Element	Less Than High Performance	High Performance
Base pay	• Tenure • Little pay differentiation for performance, skill, competence	• Reward sustained performance or value added to business over time, skill and competence
Variable pay or incentives	• None or management only • Retrospective "bonus"	• Most/all people eligible • Reward results—not all receive
Recognition and celebration	• Unaligned and/or infrequent	• Aligned with business, frequent, many types
Benefits	• Major focus • Start liberal and erode regularly • Annual cost reaction without longer-term integration	• Competitive but no more • Shared cost, affordable, keep promises • Active benefits cost management
Reward customization	• Minimal, basically all the same	• Customized based on business needs
Fairness	• Entitlement • Internal equity	• Equal opportunity to perform • Reward based on performance

EXHIBIT 1 Belief System Concerning the Total Pay Component of Total Rewards

The focus in Exhibit 3 is on the components of total rewards other than total pay—individual growth, compelling future, positive workplace—as well as the organization's response to change. All are as critical to a total rewards belief system as any elements discussed earlier.

Creating High Performance

We believe strongly that the role of pay and other rewards is to help create a true high-performance organization—one where the workforce is fully engaged in acquiring and applying critical skills and competencies to produce results and add value to the business for which they share responsibility. At one of our presentations, we were asked, "Why do both of you keep talking about creating and sustaining a high-performance organization?" Our answer remains the same as it was then: "In the 25-plus years we have been in the rewards profession, we have never had anyone request a solution with the objective of creating a poor-performing organization."

	EXHIBIT 2 **Belief System Concerning Performance Management and Management of People**	
Element	Less Than High Performance	High Performance
Goal setting	• Unlinked, very close line-of-sight goals that individual controls • Inflexible goals	• Cascading goals that individual influences—lengthening line of sight • Flexible to changing business directions
Performance management	• Everyone rated high performer • Little differentiation in evaluating performance • Focus on evaluation, not entire process	• Stretch goals with level-setting expectations • Natural differentiation based on results and competencies • Entire process is important—setting expectations, feedback, coaching, results, evaluation
Superkeepers	• Not identified	• Identify and reward those with critical skills and competencies that are translated into results—now and potential for future
Managing out poor fit/poor performers	• No honest communication • Retain too long	• Provide feedback and development • But if unsuccessful, terminate quickly and humanely for sake of all

We have organized *High-Performance Pay: Fast Forward to Business Success* into five parts. Together they tell what we believe is a useful story about how organizations can use pay and other rewards to facilitate their journey to business success.

Part I: Forging a Direction

Companies communicate business direction and values by rewarding what is important to them. In addition to business goals, one direction is to get and keep as many top performers as possible. The first chapter suggests that organizations need to develop rewards strategies geared to the high performers who generate most of the results the business needs to grow and thrive—the "superkeepers." Superkeepers are characteristic of an organization that has made itself attractive to customers, the public in

Element	Less Than High Performance	High Performance
Individual growth	• Organization's responsibility	• Individual and organization involved with individual accountable
	• Development based on interest more than business need	• Build capabilities for competitive advantage
	• Performance management is annual event without ongoing feedback and strong link to business results	• Performance management requires staying up-to-date in skill/competency and focuses on feedback and coaching
	• Career paths dominated by years of experience	• Clear career paths based on skill/competency and sustained results
Compelling future	• Job for life	• Win-win over time
	• "Make nice" for everyone	• Vision, values, directions and "deal" communicated and reinforced
Positive workplace	• "We take care of you"	• "Organization's success and your value-added provide our future"
	• Pockets of "walk the walk"	• Leadership set example and "walks the talk"
	• Work-life balance without performance required	• Work-life balance in response to business need
	• As-needed, stand-alone communications	• Clear, timely and consistent, two-way communication; listening, dialoguing
Change	• Slow/resistant to change	• Flexible to respond to changes in business direction
	• Good at planning	• Good at executing as well as planning
	• "Travel heavy," then layoffs	• "Travel light"

EXHIBIT 3 Belief System Concerning Total Rewards Other Than Total Pay

general, investors, other stakeholders and the workforce—organizations that have "branded" themselves as high performance. The second chapter suggests organizations should customize their workforce brand to be attractive to people who can thrive in, facilitate and sustain a high-performance organization. The last chapter in Part I shares ways to improve a key communication vehicle of business direction—performance management.

Chapter 1: Winning the Battle for Superkeepers

In our book, *Pay People Right!*, we posed a total rewards model and suggested total rewards can accelerate business success. High-performance organizations depend heavily on the high-performing 20 percent of the workforce for generating results—some say the high performing generate 80 percent of the results. "Superkeepers" are willing and able to acquire critical skills and competencies and translate these into measurable results—results that add value to the organization in terms of financial, customer, operational, people and future-focused outcomes. This means customizing total rewards to focus on top performers and make excellence worthwhile. With limited total rewards budgets, businesses must give first priority to these superkeepers who really make a performance difference because high-performance organizations need to attract and retain more than their share of the best talent available. The best people, the superkeepers, prefer organizations where they are rewarded for making a difference—so total rewards must make this a reality. This chapter discusses selective talent strategies, building superkeeper rewards strategies, a continuum of approaches to reward superkeepers and three case studies.

Chapter 2: Creating a Powerful Customized Workplace Rewards Brand

What a business rewards communicates to current and future workforce members what it is like to work at a particular organization. If leaders intend to form a high-performance organization with a culture of performance, the proof is in its statement about what is rewarded and recognized and its actual practices. To attract and engage a workforce that is seeking rewards based on continuous growth in competencies and skills and the resulting performance, the total rewards solution must deliver that message. We suggest that a workforce brand that is about results, performance measurement, open communication, skill and competence that add business value, growth of strong and effective talent, opportunities and career paths for growth, and a powerful win-win relationship between the organization and the workforce creates a clear message about the business focusing on high performance. The brand tells the tale and deciding on the brand for your organization is a strategic imperative.

Chapter 3: Fixing Performance Management: A Key Priority

Performance management is at the core of many elements of total rewards and the creation of a high-performance organization. Without a sound performance management program, businesses have difficulty identifying and subsequently strongly differentiating pay based on performance. We propose improvements that can be made to performance-management systems, including 10 "fixes" for enhancing effectiveness. Suggestions include goal clarity, customization to specific organizational needs, initiating culture change surrounding feedback and dialogue, engaging managers and the workforce in the process and updating as business directions change. We provide a case study and emphasize the importance of communication.

Part II: Accelerating Business Performance with Incentives

Incentives have been the core of our company's consulting practice and writings since it began more than 21 years ago. Part II leads off with a chapter on tips about incentive design that extend the research and experience we applied to develop our book, *The New Pay*. Next, the award-winning article "Revisiting Effective Incentive Design" is focused on how organizations can design incentives as the primary reward for performance. The last chapter in Part II shows incentive examples of two very important non-management, customer-focused talent teams—customer service representatives in contact centers and material handlers in distribution centers who are the last to touch the product before it reaches the customer.

Chapter 4: Powering Up Incentives for the Fast-Moving Economy

This chapter poses six principles for effectively developing or updating a total rewards system. One of these principles is to reward results with variable pay (cash or stock). We provide eight tips for incentives to drive business results, including measurable outcomes, results-focused goal setting, few key goals, meaningful upside opportunity for exceeding goals and win-win incentive opportunity. Workforcewide eligibility enables organizations to make the most of this strong communication tool. In slow- and fast-moving economies, incentives help keep people goal-oriented and proactive in making a positive performance difference.

Chapter 5: Revisiting Effective Incentive Design: Still *the* Major ROI Reward Opportunity

In *The New Pay*, we suggested that variable pay or incentives should be a preferred way to create a powerful win-win between organizations and their workforce. Since then, literally thousands of organizations have implemented variable pay below the management level with exciting results. In this chapter, we revisit the issue of incentives and variable pay and provide a business case for accelerating the journey to becoming a high-performance organization by leading this change with variable pay. Here we discuss why incentives work, how to choose measures and goals, selecting a variable pay design that matches the organization's business case for performance, putting "stretch" into goals, communication and championing, and remaining agile and flexible so incentive designs can change and adapt based on where the organization needs to go and the evolving role of the workforce in getting there. The evidence is "in" that incentives work, but keeping on course is important because business needs change, and adapting incentives to these changes produces business advantage.

Chapter 6: Best-Practice Incentives for Contact Centers and Distribution Centers: Driving Customer Satisfaction

Found in many organizations, contact centers (call centers) and distribution centers have workforces that strongly impact customer satisfaction and hence business success. This chapter, based on a survey of incentive practices, illustrates how incentive plans need to be customized based on the way work is organized and the customer interface. Individual incentives reflect the individualized customer interaction of the customer service representatives in the contact center; distribution centerwide incentives match the customers' expectation for timely delivery of the right order. Some key design principles apply to incentives in contact centers and distribution centers, such as agility in reward design, creating customer partnerships, few metrics, frequent awards and transparency to customers and the workforce.

Part III: Adding Value through Base Pay

Variable pay is a natural for rewarding performance and results, but the first chapter in Part III shows ways to get the most performance impact for base-pay increase expenditures. We have always favored paying the person rather than the job, and the second chapter in this part suggests that the time may be right for a new approach to valuing worth and positioning base pay. The third and fourth chapters address two forms of base pay—pay based on competency models that are focused on the organization's core competencies and, secondly, the assessment and the re-birth of practical and workable skill-based pay. The last chapter in Part III suggests that the time is right for skill pay to become more useable and manageable through Web-based applications that ultimately integrate with other HR programs. The combination of Parts II and III suggests that the future should be for base pay to reflect increasing value added to the business over time and variable pay and incentives to reward shorter-term performance results.

Chapter 7: Can Base Pay Reward Performance?

Can base pay be used to really reward differences in performance when it serves so many objectives? Incentives and variable pay have become the pay-for-performance tool of choice, but what about designing a base pay plan that focuses on rewarding performance? It seems probable that a combination of variable pay and base pay can get a more powerful result than just incentives alone. Base salary adjustment dollars continue to be scarce. However, organizations that are willing to go beyond the traditional treatment of base pay adjustments can get improved mileage from the largest expenditure element of total rewards—base pay. This chapter suggests eight action steps organizations can consider if they really want to reward performance and their high performers using their salary increase budgets.

Chapter 8: Measuring the Value of Work

We start with job evaluation and discuss how it has evolved and why it has been so important to the development of the total rewards field. Job evaluation organized the work-valuing process and gave organizations and workforces an orderly way to consider and value jobs. This chapter addresses available alternatives, the issue of internal and market value of jobs, and why job-valuing systems are challenged by organizations that need to be agile and adapt to meet business conditions and to take advantage of new opportunities and directions. We discuss job-valuing alternatives and suggest that additional alternatives are needed because jobs lack the agility of people and organizations are no longer able or interested in conducting elaborate job-defining and internal-valuing processes going forward. A market focus alone may not be the answer. We describe a possible new solution that addresses skill and competence as well as the external market. Calling for some new technologies and a simplified solution will make people-valuing important in high-performance organizations and in organizations that want to adapt quickly. Technology is pertinent and available. The need is for synthesis and designing a usable, business-friendly solution.

Chapter 9: Competencies and Rewards

Paying for competencies (behaviors, knowledge and skills) has significant potential but needs to reinforce a few, clearly defined, critical competencies for successful implementation. The impact of paying for competencies should be considered at the front-end of designing the organization's competency model, not on the backend, because pay decisions require assessment in a measurable, objective way. Challenges include compensation survey data based on jobs, not competencies, and business leaders accustomed to being paid through job-based, not people-based, rewards systems. The argument for paying for competencies and skills rather than jobs is that paying the person enables an organization to fine tune the labor market based on business-needed competencies and skills and reward the people who are best able to acquire and apply strategic skills and core competencies to produce results—the superkeepers. Lessons learned such as simplicity, stronger business focus and pragmatism need to be applied in implementing and updating programs that align pay with an organization's key competencies.

Chapter 10: Assessing the Value of Skill-Based Pay

We favor paying for skill and competence rather than just for jobs. The reason is that people, not jobs, are the building blocks of high-performance organizations. However, skill-based pay has had difficulty showing value-added from the investment required. Changing from paying the job to paying for skills takes time and effort and is an investment in an organization's future and the success of the workforce. This chapter discusses what can go wrong and why and how to address these issues constructively. We share criteria for effective design and questions to ask to determine if skill-based pay will work in your organization. The chapter suggests where skill-based pay can add most value in creating a more flexible, highly skilled workforce.

Chapter 11: Business Value, Paying for Skill and the Internet

We believe paying for skills can be accelerated by Internet applications. While we are not experts on Web-based total rewards technologies and systems, we know that the basic elements of a straightforward and entirely Web-based skill-based rewards system exist. Parts of it are available; and we believe that a combination of existing, modified and new technology can counteract the major administrative, management, pricing and communication challenges making skill pay less practical than it can be. All that is needed is a commitment to develop the paying-for-the-person solution that includes skill pay management, a skills/competency library and skills-profiling capability and that ultimately integrates with other HR programs—development and training, performance management and assessment, and staffing and recruitment. The business case for putting skill pay on the Web is a powerful one. And the timing for such a change is now because speed and agility are priorities that grow each day.

Part IV: Making Positive Change

"It all starts when someone sells something," and Part IV starts with a chapter about sales compensation. The success of an effective sales compensation program can facilitate extending incentives elsewhere in the enterprise. This group of chapters is a potpourri of ways to move to high performance. Executive compensation—both for profit and nonprofit—is an issue of governance and sets the example of paying for performance for the entire organization. The U.S. Postal Service (USPS) may be the best example of paying for performance and the most significant change to a performance culture we have seen in our entire careers. Finally, we show how Web products are important to the future of the total rewards field, but more innovation and more applied solutions need to be designed and brought to market.

Chapter 12: Sales Rewards Solutions

One of a company's key strategic and tactical challenges and opportunities to gain advantage is how to reward sales professionals. This chapter suggests what to review in a sales compensation plan to determine if it is meeting the needs of the business and the salesforce. Addressing six areas will provide a high-performance sales pay tune-up: providing the opportunity for competitive compensation, especially for strong performers; ensuring a proper base-incentive mix based on selling conditions; updating incentive measures and goals consistent with the business plan; setting realistic performance goals based on business conditions; updating target customers; and reinforcing critical selling behaviors and capabilities. This chapter describes significant opportunities organizations have to help the salesforce achieve stronger sales results.

Chapter 13: Executive Compensation: Doing the 'Heavy-Lifting'

High-performance organizations and rewarding performance are closely linked. Paying executives based on performance is a testimony that a performance culture exists in the organization. All stakeholders in the success of a business win when senior leadership compensation is aligned with performance—and the tools exist and fit with the new environment of greater executive compensation transparency and the need to not only cascade goals from the top to the bottom of the organi-zation but also set a positive example at the top. HR leaders must help by asking the right questions and communicating, educating and advising CEOs and boards about ensuring close alignment between organizational performance and the compensation of the most visible employees—the executives. Long-term compensation tools, such as performance shares (equity), reward based on performance. Regulations and legislation have brought executive compensation under closer scrutiny and add momentum to rewarding key leadership talent based on results.

Chapter 14: Executive Compensation within Nonprofits: Rewarding Excellence and Ensuring Governance

Governance and ethics are integral to the total rewards profession. While this chapter addresses the concerns facing nonprofit organizations relative to executive compensation, it most importantly deals with the essential objective of rewarding executive performance to make an organization high performance. The business case for rewarding executives for their performance includes everything from customer issues to alignment opportunities with the overall workforce to providing metrics that can be translated for variable pay throughout the entire organization. We build a case for board involvement and responsibility and the importance of going beyond the issues of reasonableness and competitiveness to reinforce what the organization is all about. The message is that executive rewards do not just involve how or how much the leadership team is paid—rather, executive rewards are a communication vehicle about what the organization values and what it does to reward performance and get the best talent possible.

Chapter 15: Pay for Performance Works: The U.S. Postal Service Presents a Powerful Business Case

We can think of no better testimony to the value of paying for performance than the USPS and believe any organization can use this case study for any of its workforce as part of the business case for rewarding performance. This chapter describes how USPS turned around its customer service and financial fortunes and made significant and meaningful improvements in on-time delivery, safety, productivity and every other key performance metric. The organization did this by designing and implementing a pay-for-performance program for 75,000 white-collar employees. In light of the very significant organizational turnaround with just a limited reward revolution, one must wonder what sort of outstanding results USPS would get if it implemented pay for performance for the entire workforce. USPS professionals read *The New Pay* and took the challenge to make meaningful improvements in performance by changing rewards and beginning to combat a workplace encrusted with entitlement and rewards based only on tenure. We can only think that if this move to becoming a high-performance organization can work for a government agency, can similar changes also positively impact all organizations, including the U.S. auto and airline companies?

Chapter 16: Evaluating Human Resource Pay and Rewards Computer and Web Products

Once we suggested how organizations can implement practical and effective skill and competency pay solutions as a key to better total rewards, we turned to technology for some of the important tools that can be used. However, if you walk through the technology exhibits at HR conferences, you see that most of the solutions offered for sale do not advance the knowledge base of the pay and rewards field and seem to be replicating each other. The systems available provide for record-keeping, cost management, administration, analysis and communication, and they improve accuracy. So what's the problem? The issue is that these systems are much like high-powered calculators. This chapter suggests that these systems are not ready to add value to skill pay. Available systems lack uniqueness and seem like carbon copies of each other; they do not offer better practices even though they advertise themselves as flexible. They ignore a possible educational opportunity and are only infrastructure with little content. A major problem is the instability of suppliers of these systems so committing to one system may be creating as many problems as it solves. Improvement is needed, but some are on the right track and need a small "nudge" to provide something high-performance organizations can really use.

Part V: Moving Forward

We predicted the future accurately in 1992 and are suggesting what the future holds for total pay in the next decade in the first chapter in Part V. At the center of creating the future are total rewards professionals. Our final chapter argues their importance and shares some ideas and concepts that may serve to pilot the professional through a successful career.

Chapter 17: Pay Changes Going Forward

Here we start by reviewing the recent evolution of total pay and then look forward to a positive and exciting future with predictions and requirements. We focus on total pay rather than on total rewards and outline the continuing trend to make rewards an extension of the business process and a tool of the high-performance organization. Predictions for the future are offered in the areas of base pay valuing and adjustments, incentive metrics, cash incentives, stock, recognition and celebration and benefits. The chapter summarizes some of the material presented in this book and provides a jumping-off point to what we believe will be important in the near future.

Chapter 18: Career Directions for Total Rewards Professionals

The core of the HR profession is the total rewards professional. The total rewards professional influences what typically is an organization's largest opportunity cost— total rewards. These professionals do not have a "fast track" to the top HR job. In this chapter, we build a business case for creating a total rewards profession rather than separate professions for compensation, benefits and work-life matters. The key to the future of the total rewards professional is creating high-performance organizations, and we share our idea of the central role total rewards and the total rewards professional can play in making this a reality.

The objective of *High-Performance Pay: Fast Forward to Business Success* is to challenge thinking and encourage you to develop a proactive position about using pay and other rewards to enhance organizational effectiveness and move the business forward as well as attract, motivate, retain, develop and engage the workforce.

PART I
Forging a Direction

CHAPTER 1:
Winning the Battle for Superkeepers

What will total rewards look like in the next decade? Changes are required to make total rewards a powerful tool for business leaders. Pay and rewards solutions should be directed at the top-performing 20 percent of any workforce—the critically skilled people who are uniquely able to consistently translate their skills and competencies into measurable outcomes. The contemporary total rewards program must ensure that organizations do this as a consistent talent strategy—not just when the company needs to weed out poor performers. This value comes in the form of total rewards.

Essential employees are *superkeepers* who comprise the talent that makes a business successful. Although many companies are replacing high-paid employees with low-paid employees whenever possible, they need a strategy that rewards generously for talent that adds real business value. A best-of-the-best talent rewards solution puts substance into the business case for paying for performance.

The challenge is the gap that exists between what business leaders know is the optimal policy and what they actually do, as is the case with the realities of pay and rewards. Although leaders know their organization is most likely to be successful if it rewards superkeepers, they do not completely connect good intentions with implementation.

How are superkeepers different from scarce talent? Superkeepers are more important than scarce talent. A scarce-talent environment exists when the demand for people with skills exceeds the supply. Market scarcity of high market-value skills may change over time. When market scarcity exists, organizations must pay a premium for people who are scarce talent. Although some superkeepers may not even have skills that are scarce in the general marketplace, they have capabilities and a performance record that are critical to the organization's mission.

Superkeeper Strategy

A superkeeper strategy is a broad talent strategy that defines the roles employees will play in making organizations a success. It gives priority to identifying and rewarding employees for performance by revitalizing many HR tools, including total rewards, performance management, training and development, succession planning, selection and placement, coaching and mentoring. In the superkeeper context, they become the money tools that credibly identify and reward key contributors.

Organizations need to review how closely their rewards solution aligns with the company's business strategy. Most companies execute talent strategies and corresponding rewards strategies that are not equipped to deal with the real-world skill and performance challenges.

'Spread Cream Cheese' Strategy

The "spread cream cheese" analogy refers to a senior manager who said her company's rewards strategy was to spread rewards "as evenly as cream cheese on a bagel." The company shared pay and rewards dollars without consistently determining which employees add the best value. The manager's frustration was rooted in the absence of a way to identify, reward, recognize and retain the most critical employees when the company operated on a reduced budget and was forced to reduce its workforce.

This company's rewards strategy worked well in good times but was inflexible when business fortunes ebbed and flowed. Being named to a "best place to work" list doesn't require a company to show it has a rewards solution agile enough to bend with periodic downhill business gyrations. An entitlement-oriented rewards program fails to prepare the workforce for hard times. And the deal breaker is people with the highest skills and performance receive little more than poorer performers.

Queen of Hearts Strategy

In Lewis Carroll's *Alice in Wonderland*, the Queen of Hearts is notorious for ordering the beheading of subjects who offend her. Some formerly exalted companies found themselves unprepared to manage talent based on how people add value. They faced a need to reward performance and reduce headcount. But the CEOs did not wait for the tools to be in place to really do performance management and pay for performance. Rather, the tool of the moment was commonly some sort of performance ranking by managers who were unprepared to make objective and realistic talent judgments. This often carried dire consequences for the company's reputation and its talent pool.

Because more than a few companies lack viable talent support systems such as coaching, rater training and valid performance tools, most attempts to identify critical talent were haphazard at best. This resulted in poor preparation in the arena of performance standards and goal setting and incomplete training of managers to judge skill and performance or how to handle pay and rewards. In addition, there were major lapses in communications to the workforce about skill and competency expectations and performance standards detailing how employees are expected to turn what they know into outcomes.

The Queen of Hearts strategy does not create a win-win culture. Often, it has a highly negative impact on the company talent pool and sometimes brands the company as one that treats people harshly. Such solutions fail to create a superkeeper talent strategy. In some instances, the result is accusations of discrimination. In other instances, organizations must reinstate employees who were terminated through the application of tools that unfairly identified and applied the talent criteria.

Lessons about Superkeepers

Talent strategy experiences teach companies much about the journey to total rewards. It is clear that a positive work environment, compelling future, individual growth and total pay are the right building blocks for total rewards. Organizations are branding and customizing their total rewards packages to communicate what it is like to work there. Total rewards can make companies attractive. The lesson learned from the "spread the cream cheese" and Queen of Hearts discussions is companies need to get maximum value from investments in total rewards. This has the best chance of occurring when rewards focus on superkeepers.

Just providing liberal pay and benefits and evenly distributing rewards to everyone has no track record of making a company an employer of preference for top-performing employees. Instead, a company must pay for essential skills and competencies and the ability to deploy these to achieve goals. It is necessary to have valid tools and systems in place to credibly judge talent. Too often, statements of talent strategic intent are so general that nobody could possibly dispute them.

Selective Talent Strategies

Making a company a best place to work means placing a priority on skill and performance. Exhibit 1-1 compares and contrasts rewards strategies. Superkeeper talent strategies are business strategies. Many talent strategies are not selective. All organizations hope to attract employees, but their talent strategies often do not

EXHIBIT 1-1 **Comparing Total Rewards Strategies**	
Most Rewards Strategies	**Superkeeper Rewards Strategies**
• Element of only HR strategy	• Element of business strategy
• Rewards driven by equity and fairness	• Rewards focus on business needs first
• Constant from year to year	• Adapt as talent needs evolve
• Rewards attractive to all	• Rewards most attractive to superkeepers
• Uniform competitive practice for all skills and jobs	• Strongly competitive for superkeepers
• Questionable performance link	• Close performance tie-in

target superkeepers. Companies should build a talent strategy around this element of the workforce by taking the following steps:

- **Encourage some employees to leave.** A *WorldatWork* conference keynote speaker, Curt Coffman, asked several chief executives how long it took them to tell if a new employee was a keeper. The most frequent response was less than one month. When asked how long it took to get rid of someone who did not fit, the more frequent answer was more than 10 years. Many organizations make it more attractive for substandard performers to stay. Most leaders agree that employees who do not add value should leave and find a better fit elsewhere.

- **Reward to grow.** Keepers comprise about 80 percent of an organization's workforce and make it a success. This talent has important skills and competencies, some of which may be scarce in the external marketplace. The scarce nature of their skills provides them with a marketplace-rewards premium. The organization needs a strategy to keep the best of this keeper group and raise the performance and talent bar for these employees. They are one possible source of superkeepers, but they are not the best skilled and most talented in the organization. It is the group that is important from the standpoint of designing the rewards, performance management, training, coaching and feedback tools that encourage development, growth and performance.

- **Reward superkeepers above all.** The talent and total rewards strategy should focus on rewarding superkeepers, making it attractive for them to stay and continue to perform at an excellent level. It has been said that 20 percent of employees achieve 80 percent of the results. If this is true, the superkeepers are in the top 20 percent. Other capable employees should be encouraged to perform and join this select pool.

If a company cannot develop valid criteria for mission-essential talent and define what performance is in credible terms, it will be impossible to implement a superkeeper talent strategy. A process for identifying the key talent is shown in Exhibit 1-2. It provides a possible foundation for problem-solving talent strategies. Organizations have the option of implementing the same rewards programs throughout the company or customizing them to match differences that may exist across organizational business units. These business units may have substantially different superkeeper needs in terms of defining mission-essential skill and competency as well as how performance will be measured (see Exhibit 1-3).

Total Rewards Tools

Talent tools include recruitment, selection and placement solutions that support the superkeeper definitions developed to match the business plan. They also include performance and skill/competency assessment tools that really work. These tools are geared toward implementing clear talent objectives, criteria for measuring and encouraging them, and supporting systems that enable the organization to staff itself consistent with its talent goals.

EXHIBIT 1-2 Identifying Superkeepers and Responding to Their Needs

1. What skills/competencies are absolutely needed?
2. Which people have these skills/competencies?
3. Which people can translate skills/competencies into business outcomes?
4. Where are more people who fit this mold now?
5. What rewards do they want and in what balance—individual growth, compelling future, positive workplace or total pay?
6. What rewards changes need to be made?
7. Is your company ready or willing to make the changes?

EXHIBIT 1-3 Allow for Customization Within the Organization

Same Rewards Programs Across Company	Custom Rewards Programs—More Autonomy
Core business	Different industry/different competitors
Similar jobs	Different jobs
Similar labor market	Different labor market
Centralized	Decentralized
People transfer between business units	Little transfer between business units

The company must develop training and talent plans that are capable of keeping talent current. This means constantly updating the business needs for skills and competencies. The most important need is the development of managers who coach and develop talent. All of these more effective systems are intended elements of most contemporary HR management strategies. However, the premium being placed on employees who are essential to the business in superkeeper talent strategies requires that these tools be honed to their finest edge of effectiveness.

The Proof

Three case studies help prove the point: Talent strategies are driven by business needs. Each scenario depicts a problem that resulted in a customized rewards solution. All had incorporated agility and flexibility so they could change as needed. None of the solutions involved liberal pay and benefits for the entire workforce. They also avoided poorly engineered attempts to identify key talent that resulted in arbitrary and unfair decisions that did more harm than good.

Consumer products company. This company was performing acceptably, but the talent strategy called for better workforce alignment with goals and improved emphasis on the people who made a real performance difference. Management believed that if employees had some skin in the game, it would help. The solution was to evaluate how well employees' base pay matched employees' value to the organization. Criteria building preceded this process, as did communications about what constitutes a superkeeper in this organization. The rewards goal was to strengthen the relationship between superkeeper status and pay standing. Reviewing pay in relation to value prompted the company to undertake a realignment effort.

Superkeeper identification involved fitting people into one of three categories— (1) must keep or primary superkeepers, (2) not want to lose (but not must keep) or secondary superkeepers and (3) others who are important to keep the business running effectively but not superkeepers. Sample criteria included criticality to success of business during the next few years, unique skills or experiences, the company's ability to replace the individual if necessary and having a critical core role or core competencies required by the business.

Base-pay management changed to grant pay increases based on value added to the business. The determination was based on a dollar amount and not percentage increase. The process was to review total compensation (base pay and short- and long-term variable pay) to ensure all pay dollars are effectively spent. Managers were trained and accountable for budget and retaining people with high superkeeper status.

The lesson here is that manager accountability for superkeeper retention drives pay differentiation. Managers were trained to pay based on overall value to the organization. It required talking honestly with employees about superkeeper status and what they need to do to increase their value to the business.

High-technology company. The high-tech industry was in the doldrums when this case developed. The company had a limited base pay increase budget and underwater stock options. It started with a careful analysis to identify core competencies of the business that include those that help differentiate the business from its competitors. This yardstick was used to train managers to coach and select superkeepers who are critical to the business and strong performers. In this instance, they were almost exclusively technology people. The focus was on nonmanagement employees with the talent the business determined was mission critical. Two judgments were subsequently made about the risk of losing superkeepers:

• Their marketability in the competitive labor market.

• Employee satisfaction with the company and the components of total rewards.

The company determined early that base pay increase budgets were too small to make a difference. They had a performance management process that was capable of applying the newly developed measures of criticality and performance. The focus was on cash incentive opportunity that varied based on criticality of superkeeper status rather than level in the organization, as it was prior to this effort. The combination of opportunity plus basing the award on achieving individual goals rewarded not only superkeeper talent skills but also the ability to translate them into performance results. The performance management system made this real for the employees.

The lesson here is that flexibility counts. The company moved from base pay to incentives based on skill differences and the ability to perform individually. The outcome of superkeeper identification driven by pay needs gave momentum to succession planning and long-term workforce development. It was part of a migration to a total rewards solution focused on value to the business.

Telecommunications company. This company was in serious distress. Survival was the goal with a key workforce of essential talent needed for turning the business around. The search for top performers in key roles with essential talent identified key finance and customer relationship skills as superkeeper talent. In this case, it amounted to a superkeeper cadre of less than 10 percent of the total workforce. The company had a highly selective talent strategy focused specifically on getting the company across a difficult economic bridge with the key talent it needed to remain a company.

The solution was a retention bonus for the 10 percent of the workforce needed. It was designed in installment payments with the largest payment at the end of company restructuring. Keeping the talent pool intact was the goal. This solution replaced the loss of regular incentives and stock options. Also, the company added an enhanced severance program as protection if these essential people were let go in the future. Terminating old programs and replacing them with a solution focused directly on the situation was key in this case.

The lesson here is that old programs just will not work under a company survival mode. These programs were developed during different times and under different sets of assumptions about the company's future. This company needed a highly proactive program to focus critical people on the business. The burning platform does make the superkeeper strategy much easier to implement than would be possible when times are good and pay and incentives are plentiful.

Developing Superkeeper Total Rewards

These cases suggest that companies can consider a continuum of rewards approaches for superkeepers. Exhibit 1-4 lists the possible solutions. Some of these alternatives are fairly transparent, so we will emphasize those that need some discussion.

At Level 1, the company creates greater differentiation in base-pay adjustments based on value added on an individual basis. It needs support tools for the performance process and compares individual value to actual pay and implements a strategy to correct the difference. At Level 2, a portion of any base pay increase budget goes additionally to superkeepers only. A 1-percent allocation means 5 percent additional to 20 percent superkeepers or it means 10 percent if the company has 10 percent superkeepers. In Level 3, superkeepers are provided an additional cash variable pay opportunity. This can be linked to or separate from the ongoing performance management process. Many incentive choices are possible,

---

EXHIBIT 1-4 Continuum of Approaches for Superkeepers

Level 1. Greater differentiation in base-pay increase budget

Level 2. Allocate portion of base-pay dollars to superkeepers only

Level 3. Additional variable pay

Level 4. Additional stock vehicles

Level 5. Total compensation—past, present, future

Level 6. Total rewards

such as an additional annual incentive opportunity, special recognition awards or project incentives. The performance periods can be flexible to respond to the specific business situation.

For Level 4, additional stock vehicles can be offered to superkeepers. The perceived value of options varies from company to company. Restricted stock has retention value and may be an alternative to options. Performance shares are worth evaluation because they have both retention and performance value. In Level 5, we have a total compensation solution that communicates to each individual on a single page what they have: base, short- and long-term variable pay, additional compensation and so on. Job changes to gain skills and competencies and recognition of significant achievements can be part of the formula. In Level 6, the total rewards solution involves more than total pay and provides the most customized superkeeper solution of all.

Practical for Any Company

Companies need to be ready for superkeeper rewards solutions. The time is right for considering changes to how people are rewarded. Organizations need a strategy that outlines the solutions suggested in this book, such as the following:
- Identify superkeepers with critical skills who generate measurable outcomes.
- Focus a rewards strategy on getting and keeping core talent.
- Build a rewards strategy that makes being a superkeeper attractive.
- Design and implement the systems and tools needed to make the superkeeper talent strategy a reality.

If a company wants to proceed, what steps should it take to get from its present rewards strategy to where the business requires rewards to be? The initial step is to diagnose the existing situation. What is the current state compared to what it needs to be? Ask these questions:
- What are the organization's talent and skill needs based on its business strategy and goals?
- Is the organization clear about how to define superkeepers?
- Does the organization have the tools to identify superkeepers in a valid and reliable fashion?
- Is the organization prepared to nurture and develop talent in a superkeeper strategy?
- What does the superkeeper talent pool want that is unique from what others want?
- What total rewards will help the organization get and keep the superkeeper talent they need?

Armed with the answers, the next step is to strategize how to do this, develop and implement the programs, then communicate and train. Training is imperative because managers are the primary communicators and need tools to do this effectively. Managers actively review superkeepers quarterly and are responsible for results so they also must be accountable for people and rewards to ensure value added. Finally, it is critical to continually evaluate the program for improvement as the company situation and plans change.

The Future

Company leaders urgently want a powerful business case for rewards. They want to see where their dollars are spent. Leaders realize that some talent is more critical to the company than others. The future should emphasize more business alignment. The ability to get and keep the best people with critical skills is a continuing opportunity for all companies. Wise companies will move to become increasingly willing to implement rewards with a bias to critical talent. This offers a great opportunity to differentiate your company from others. The solution is becoming more evident, and the next few years will tell us who is best positioned for the next decade.

First published in *Compensation & Benefits Review*, March/April 2004, 36 (2), 38-44. Reprinted by permission of SAGE Publications Inc.

CHAPTER 2:
Creating a Powerful Customized Workplace Rewards Brand

What is in a name? Ask the likes of Pepsi, Coke, General Mills, BMW and Disney—it is customer holding power. A top brand name delivers lots of it. Company name recognition really counts. A familiar and notable product or service brand that invokes a recall of positive experiences gets the attention of customers. Without a recognizable brand, advertising dollars focused on capturing customers are wasted. Workplace brands are geared toward the same thing—attracting the people a company wants and needs to be a success. Companies require effective product and workplace branding.

Southwest Airlines and General Electric created workplace brands to support their product and service brand. Although widely different, these brands define the types of people they require. These companies provide a special work environment as a magnet to employees who fit their workforce model—the model that describes the work characteristics of persons that succeed in these businesses. Custom workplace branding lets people know what it is like to work in the company. Having a workplace brand, top companies suggest, often leads to gaining customer advantage. If people like the company they work for, they will reflect this in how they treat customers.

Unique Workplace Brands

Companies spend billions annually on HR programs and initiatives. This expenditure is comparable to other major business investments. But does the organization get maximum mileage in terms of workforce trust and commitment from this cost? Workplace branding may give companies the best chance to maximize their return in terms of investment in their people.

The workplace, career, employment or other custom-brand designation should make the company attractive to the people the company wants. As advertising products and services attempts to suggest unique value to targeted customers, workplace branding intends to make the company unique to employees. Branding makes a positive statement about what it is like to work for a company, and it communicates what people can expect in the future. A company can advertise a name workplace brand rather than a generic brand.

Workplace branding is not new. "Employers of choice" and "best places to work" designations by *Fortune* and *Working Mother* acknowledge companies that are successful in developing a highly positive workplace. These workplace-branded companies go the extra mile to ensure that everyone, with emphasis on people below the management levels, experiences an attractive work situation.

Our review of the *Fortune* and *Working Mother* best companies suggests they share a number of characteristics in common. Most critically, these companies

- are family friendly,
- provide liberal benefits,
- support education,
- are diversity biased,
- are somewhat egalitarian,
- emphasize collaboration and
- provide something distinguished about the workplace.

"Best places" usually provide fairly uniform benefits and perquisites from top to bottom. For example, executive parking, dining rooms, special retirement plans and the like are less common among companies seeking this distinction. They also tend to emphasize collaboration and participation or worker involvement to gather input or help make decisions. All have something special for their employees, ranging from day care and sabbatical leaves to a special ergonomic chair, exercise facilities and pet insurance. They try to distinguish themselves and make people an important ingredient in their formula.

Who Is Branding Your Workplace?

You do not need to be a Baldrige winner to provide quality, and you do not need to be selected as a best place to work to offer a positive workplace. At issue with these best places is who does the workplace branding for your company? *Fortune* and *Working Mother* provide inclusion criteria and guidelines for potential participants to follow. Although it is helpful to have a workplace brand confirmed by a prestigious magazine, the actual branding must cascade from the company's business goals rather than an external source.

The workplace brands typified by *Fortune* and *Working Mother* provide many of the elements of total rewards shown in opportunities for individual growth, a compelling future, a positive workplace and total pay components, including base and variable pay, benefits and recognition. The brand is supportive and positive and geared toward attracting a quality workforce that is often characterized by good morale and reasonable turnover. This workplace design has proven to be highly attractive to a very wide range of people, many of whom possess scarce and business-critical skills companies need to thrive.

These are clearly priorities for making a workplace attractive in good and less-than-excellent company performance times. However, it is essential to ensure that your workplace features will not be cast off when financial performance is not entirely satisfactory. "Best places to work" and "employer of preference" designations were established during some of the most fruitful business times of the past 20 years. These benefits must not be just fair-weather friends that disappear when business slows. Imagine the negative implications from an announcement such as, "Because of lagging financial performance, our company must suspend providing a family-friendly work environment and work-life balance for the time being. We are sure that once our financial performance has improved, we will be in a position to provide these benefits again."

Why Brand Your Workplace?

Fortune and *Working Mother* "best companies" focus on making the company attractive to everyone who has the skill and talent to work there. They say little about employee obligations to perform to company standards—and they say nearly nothing about a win-win between company and workforce. If you review the list of what these companies tend to offer, they make themselves attractive to any qualified employee. Once an employee is with the organization, it tries to retain them. This makes an organization very appealing but implies a more costly and liberal pay and rewards solution characteristic of companies not always strongly focused on developing unique workforce environments.

Some say merely providing extremely liberal benefits attracts only people interested in a comfortable workplace, one in which results and personal growth are not priorities. On the other hand, companies that really emphasize performance-based reward elements such as incentives and performance shares may have a different workplace brand. They will tell you that their performance-based brand makes them attractive principally to people interested in working in a performance culture rather than one driven only by attractive benefits.

The most powerful reason for branding is to make your company uniquely attractive, specifically to people with characteristics and capabilities in which you have interest. In other words, you should specify those who match your specific workforce model. This means putting in place what the people you want would view as important to influencing them to join and stay. This discourages people from joining you with expectations that you will not be able or do not elect to meet. This is critical for long-term workforce relationships. There is no sense in hiring or keeping people who do not match your expectations—it is unfair to everyone.

Business Performance Culture Branding

Any positive workplace brand is valuable. Following the "best companies" model is well worthwhile. Companies should go beyond providing a nice place to work. The components of total rewards should additionally take on a performance culture bias that provides advantage to both the business and the workforce.

Workplace brands should ensure the employee and the organization are winners—a win-win on both sides of the employment deal. No company is going to continue an HR strategy that does not prove to add value to the business over time. This means the components of total rewards—compelling future, individual growth, positive workplace and total pay—are geared toward creating a true performance culture. In such a workplace, people add increasing value to the enterprise's business as stakeholders and subsequently share as stakeholders according to their contribution to organizational measures of success.

Additional ingredients are necessary to create a performance culture workplace brand. Some of these are worth a bit of explaining. Specifically, companies should do the following:

- **Emphasize results.** Reinforce the culture by a workplace brand designed to be attractive to people focused on both generating measurable outcomes that add value to the business and personal growth in necessary business skills. They are not risk adverse and want to be rewarded for their performance.
- **Deploy clear business metrics throughout.** Use measures and goals for rewards that are based on the business. People are helped to understand how they add value to the business and how they should perform, and they should be provided with tools to perform effectively.
- **Provide open communication concerning expectations.** Provide information required to understand the business and the role of the workforce in creating business success. People have the information they need to do their jobs.
- **Emphasize skill and competency the business needs.** Build a learning process

around skill that is essential to the business of the enterprise. Link pay growth to the acquisition and application of these skills.

- **Develop a strong "bench."** Create backup talent for key roles and responsibilities. Have a succession plan that permits backup to be grown so the talent reservoir is sufficiently deep and effective.
- **Provide clear career paths.** Provide a route for people to follow so they can become more valuable to your company. People are worth more when they learn more. The company should provide the opportunity for workers to improve through their own efforts.
- **Implement win-win rewards.** Ensure that both sides of the workforce deal come out ahead if goals are met and people help reach these goals. It makes no sense to have rewards that do not reward both sides of a workplace brand.

Why do this? Why create a performance culture workplace brand? Because it communicates to prospective and current employees what it is like at your company. It declares that you have a specific way of doing business and requires that you define this for your people. It says you use business metrics to judge how everyone is doing so that performance counts at all levels. The message is that you do not just have jobs people do, you have skills you need, and you want people to acquire them to get necessary business results.

It states that you want excellent people growing all the time, and you provide a track that helps them grow in the directions you must go. And the bottom line is that the company will share success, and lack of success, with the people who continue to fit the model. It is the best way to make clear the rules of the road when someone joins your company team.

The most important distinction has to do with the workplace model that the performance culture brand creates for the organization. Although the more typical branded workplace is attractive to every potential employee, the performance culture model is likely to be most attractive to candidates who are more willing to have their performance evaluated and who can work in a performance culture where business measures and goals are used to make people stakeholders in company success.

Workplace Branding for Your Company?

Companies can follow a wide range of possible courses relative to how they manage HR matters. Branding makes sense for your products and services and for your workplace. How far your company elects to go is clearly a subject of business strategy and direction. But logic suggests that the only reason to brand products or workplaces is to make the business more successful. In turn, this success should be shared with those who make it a reality.

Is branding for you? You are providing a work environment of some sort for your people—that is obvious. It is also true that your company wants to provide a workplace that satisfies your people and encourages trust, commitment and even effective performance. Matching the best place workforce models is clearly a place to start, but going one step further and branding your workplace with high performance adds value to the business.

First published in *Compensation & Benefits Review*, November/December 2001, 33 (6), 30-33. Reprinted by permission of SAGE Publications Inc.

CHAPTER 3:
Fixing Performance Management: A Key Priority

With limited pay-adjustment budgets, organizations continue to be deeply challenged to use scarce adjustment dollars wisely. Recently we participated in a teleconference about predicted pay budgets. Most participants predict a limited pool for next year. When we asked what the biggest challenge was for such a limited budget, many said that it was getting the dollars to the people who deserve them the most. "We just can't reward performance or get pay adjustments to the people with the most critical skills we need." When asked why, the universal answer was, "Our performance management tools don't work. They do not effectively identify the people with the critical skills and those who perform the best."

If your organization had a valid and reliable way to evaluate individual employee performance, it would be possible to keep the best-performing employees and to deliver what raise money you have to the top performers. Without a viable performance management system, your organization can only retreat to keeping the people with the most service, with little or no regard for who is a top performer and who is a marginal performer. And we all know that service and performance are not always the same thing.

An Essential Performance Management Fix?

If you want to fix performance management for good, here are 10 suggestions that may make sense in your organization:

1. Define "performance" clearly.
2. Engage managers in helping you improve present practices.
3. Customize to your organization.
4. Provide role models.
5. Initiate culture change to support honest feedback and dialogue.
6. Update and post performance goals as directions change.
7. Engage employees in the performance management process.
8. Train raters and ratees.
9. Bring performance management out of the closet.
10. Communicate and coach.

Before we briefly summarize each suggestion, it is important to remember that performance management is much more than a forms-design exercise. If you have a solid performance management process, the forms document it. It is the goal setting, feedback, coaching, review, discussion and exchange of performance information that makes for top-notch performance management. We have clients that have excellent performance management solutions but only one piece of paper— they call it "the annual piece of paper." The focus is on the dialogue about performance because they believe, as we do, that this is where the "beef" of performance improvement and pay determination is.

One Company's Experience

This successful consumer products company with a workforce of 800 had a history of avoiding performance management to the point where employees' reviews could be six to 12 months late. Although employees got retroactive increases, they were starting to ask for interest on the retroactive increases. A lengthy, very detailed performance review form with criteria that did not seem relevant and a culture that let managers be too busy for performance management reinforced the avoidance problem. Leadership decided that fixing performance management could accelerate business significantly.

The organization had just developed a clear business strategy with key organizational goals that it wanted to cascade to the workforce to engage them in successfully achieving these goals. A design team was appointed to develop a new performance management program and process. This was a key ingredient of the new business strategy. The design team got extensive feedback from managers and employees about the new process and form. The process and supporting materials were simplified and made applicable to all employees— the form graphically shows how the employee's goals cascade from the organization's stated goals. Individual development and competencies specific to the organization's values round out the performance criteria.

Training, coaching and quarterly performance updates are key. To kick-start the process, managers had a week with no team or department meetings to work on performance management—HR staffed a room for a week where they coached managers through the performance review process and hired a writer to help managers document their thoughts. Employees also did self-evaluations to facilitate the process. The organization had a drawing that all employees whose managers completed their performance review process on time were eligible for. Because of employees' excitement about the drawing, managers got the message that the culture had changed to valuing a timely and quality performance management process. It worked and became a true high-performance performance management solution.

Three review cycles later, the company no longer needed the drawing for weekend cruises. The performance management process has become "the way it is done here."

The 10 Performance Management Priorities

Here is what organizations on the leading edge of best practice focus on during the development of their performance management process:

1. **Define "Performance" Clearly.** What is performance in your organization? How do you want to evaluate the performance of your employees? This may depend on what you are planning to do with the results of performance management. Some choices are identification of development and training needs, eligibility for promotion and transfer, pay adjustments, incentive awards, eligibility for new temporary assignments, and the like. Are you going to pay for only objective performance that is quantitative? Sales? Costs? Quality and accuracy? Customer satisfaction? Or will you also be measuring more subjective forms of performance that, while not objectively measurable, are observable—e.g., teamwork, communication and creativity? If you use any combination of measures, you must make sure they are indeed measurable, that differences in performance can be determined, and that what you are measuring really makes a difference to your organization.

2. **Engage Managers in Helping You Improve Present Practices.** Managers will become more involved in performance management if they have input into how the process works. Ask them to answer the following questions and then help you make modifications to the process as needed:

   - How is the performance management process being used across the organization?
   - What specifically about current practice is sound and what needs improvement?
   - Is the process using measures and goals that are important to your organization? Is it measuring the right performance, or too little and too late?
   - Does it have credibility, reliability and validity? Credibility with those using it is essential—do users believe it actually evaluates performance fairly?
   - Does it measure what it is supposed to measure each time it is applied?
   - If an employee asks why you are using this process, can you answer in a business-focused fashion?
   - Are you moving to a system change because the current system is not working or because it is not used?

   Once these questions are answered, managers can help you make the program more workable and meaningful to them and employees, as well as the organization.

3. **Customize to Your Organization.** Every organization is different. Two

hospitals are different. Two charities are different. Two high-tech companies differ, and so forth. The messages about performance will differ from organization to organization. Some organizations have a strong entitlement mentality that is hard to change. Others are very entrepreneurial and have difficulty with formal systems of any kind. Many have had a host of performance management solutions, and none has proven of value to the organization over time. It is not a one-size-fits-all situation, and you must match the solution to where your organization is now and where it wants to go and to how managers and employees feel about performance management. The solution needs to be owned by your organization. It makes no difference if it works elsewhere. It is great to have a solution that has a track record of success, but your organization most certainly will have different results with the same solution than will other organizations.

4. **Provide Role Models.** Performance management requires examples and sponsors. Those who sponsor performance management must be involved in the process. The most senior executive needs board review of his or her performance. And this executive must review the performance of direct reports. The performance management process cascades from top to bottom. The person who is the champion of performance management has to be a user and customer of performance management. The measures and goals need to cascade from the top of the organization to the bottom. Leaders must use the performance management process on their managers, and managers must have experience with measurement. Everyone requires feedback and coaching experience so they can add value to the process. Excellent users of the process should teach others, and the entire process depends on support by the very top people.

5. **Initiate Culture Change to Support Honest Feedback and Dialogue.**
For some organizations, a culture change is in order, particularly if managers think they do not have time for performance management or believe that to be liked or to keep easy working relationships, they cannot give constructive feedback to employees. A key managerial responsibility is developing talent, including giving feedback and coaching employees in a supportive but honest way. Role modeling by senior leadership accelerates the culture change.
You can help this change by communicating clearly upfront that one of the objectives of the improved performance management process is changing the culture. Most people want to be relevant to the organization, and goal setting related to organizational goals and performance feedback—including celebration

of successes—make them feel like the time they spend with the organization is worthwhile. The change can also be couched in terms of a development focus where everyone can improve, just like your organization's continuous improvement processes for the business. Most people want to stay up-to-date in skills and competencies, especially if they are interested in long-term career growth and employability.

You can emphasize the importance of the change by adding sound performance management as a goal or competency in every manager's performance review.

6. **Update and Post Performance Goals as Directions Change.** Make sure performance management forms do not stay in the drawer until the end of the year by providing a process to revise and update measures and goals as business directions change. Posting organizational, departmental, team and individual goals on department bulletin boards or on your organization's intranet keeps goal achievement at the forefront. People like to track how they are doing, and updating performance progress keeps the focus.

7. **Engage Employees in the Performance Management Process.** Engage employees through their participation in the process. A self evaluation before the performance review helps employees get a better perspective of their performance. Employees also increase their ownership in the process by scheduling their performance-update sessions that involve discussing progress, resources needed to achieve goals and development ideas. Encourage employees to take the lead on preparing and implementing their own development plans.

8. **Train Raters and Ratees.** Performance management is only as effective as those who apply it. It is a two-way street to get good performance management. Everyone is a ratee, and many are both raters and ratees. So, you must give people experience on both ends of the process. It takes education about the why and how of performance management. People must understand the measures and criteria to be used, and how to use the tools of the process, and, perhaps most importantly, have experience doing the performance management process: getting feedback and help as the process goes on. Coaching the coaches. Keeping the process going and making sure it is applied consistently from manager to manager and from employee to employee. Critique the process and improve how it is being applied. Managers who are good at performance management and coaching can help train and coach other managers.

9. **Bring Performance Management Out of the Closet.** Organizations that are best in performance management make sure managers are "on the same page"

by opening up the process. They get input about employee performance from others knowledgeable about the employee's performance. Managers at a similar organizational level or in a similar functional area get together to discuss the performance of employees with whom they have had contact. They dialogue about what makes outstanding performance so they come to a common ground about calibrating performance levels and "how high the performance bar is set." You can start this process by working with the senior leadership team as they review the performance of the level below them.

10. **Communicate and Coach.** If you do not communicate why this process is used and why it adds value, it will not work. And this must be ongoing communications. Do not just get everyone into an auditorium and show them a slick presentation. Communicate day by day and week after week. Talk about why the measures are important and how an employee is doing—where can they improve and what is in it for them if they do. And coaching is critical. The goal of performance management is to improve the performance of the entire organization. It is not just a performance documentation solution; it is a way to provide the information upon which real organizational performance improvement will occur.

Do these suggestions seem obvious to you? Well, research on performance management effectiveness indicates that these 10 priorities would save organizations a lot of time during the performance-management repair process. Take a look at your performance management solution and see how it stacks up compared to our suggestions.

Conclusions

We start many of our conference workshops asking what are the two major challenges HR leaders face in addressing pay for performance. No. 1 is nearly always the deficiencies of performance management. No. 2 is most often a realization that merit pay does not work because they are not able to identify performance differences upon which to differentiate pay. How much more evidence do we need before giving some attention to performance management and pay? For most organizations, pay costs are the most significant opportunity expense. So a little emphasis on making the process of distributing pay based on real performance is something to consider now.

Reprinted from *PIHRAScope*, July 2004, XLVII (7), 6-7 and 16-18, a bimonthly publication of the Professionals in Human Resources Association.

PART II

Accelerating Business Performance with Incentives

CHAPTER 4:
Powering Up Incentives
for the Fast-Moving Economy

When your employees open their paychecks each week, what signals are they getting from you? If your company is still paying its workforce based on obsolete pay solutions, you could be squelching work performance, decreasing motivation and flattening the bottom line. Are you really paying for performance or for something else? The new hyper-fast economy demands new rewards solutions. Here are some tips on how to bring home the performance bacon.

A New Look at Pay

Pay is not the only factor that motivates, but it is a very powerful way for a company to communicate its values, direction, performance expectations, standards of quality and customer satisfaction. Pay must be aligned with the business so it can effectively deliver the proper messages. In our fast-moving economy, rewards are the critical factor in enhancing workforce performance.

This new business strategy of providing total rewards—which include all compensation, a positive workplace, individual growth opportunities and a compelling future—stimulates and communicates company excellence to the workforce. A company's total rewards strategy and its reasons for changing its pay plan should be unique to that company's specific situation.

For instance, a company that produces toys at low cost may provide lower base pay to keep fixed costs low, offer variable pay that optimizes cost and quality, and use ample recognition to celebrate successes. On the other hand, a high-tech, start-up company planning an initial public offering may emphasize variable pay through stock options to invest its cash in product development. In an IPO, speed to market with a unique product or service is critical, so there is less emphasis in total rewards on fixed base pay and benefits.

A company's organizational design also affects how a total rewards strategy should work. A highly centralized company may need to provide similar types of rewards across business units and variable pay linked to overall company performance. By contrast, a virtual organization, in which there are few boundaries between the company, suppliers and customers, may be able to offer more flexible rewards.

Regardless of size or type of business, however, all companies developing a new total rewards system should follow six principles:

1. Create a positive and natural rewards experience so employees will understand, accept, support and commit to the new rewards system. It is important to involve the workforce in the reward design process through focus groups or design teams. Companies such as Monsanto and General Electric have incorporated this principle and have successfully won the support of their workforces.

2. Align rewards with business goals to create a win-win partnership for the company and its workforce. The company must provide clear direction to the workforce on how growth and profit benefit everyone. People's rewards must be linked to team, site, business unit, group or company goals and results.

3. Extend people's line of sight by making their pay the connection to key measures of business success, such as company financial performance and customer satisfaction. People want to know what the company expects of them and how they fit in the overall plan for company success. Asking them to focus only on goals that are a few feet in front of them creates a dislodged workforce, because they will not understand the company's overall objectives.

4. Integrate rewards by taking an overall perspective of total rewards, such as base pay, variable pay, benefits, an exciting and challenging work environment, the opportunity to work with excellent colleagues and leaders, individual growth opportunities and other forms of rewards the company may use. People work for more than money. It is essential to integrate all the rewards so that people understand the role they play in making the business a success and how they will share in that success.

5. Reward individual, ongoing value with base pay. To determine an individual's value, take three things into consideration: the skills and competencies the individual has that the company needs, the individual's sustained performance or track record over time and the individual's value in the labor market. Ongoing value differs from current or yearly performance, because it takes into account the individual's performance trend over time relative to current base pay. Current or annual performance and results are better addressed through variable pay, because awards can be meaningful in size and do not become an annuity for a single year's performance. A one-size-fits-all pay solution simply does not work.

6. Reward results with variable pay (cash incentives or equity). Variable pay is the key pay communication tool for linking employees to customer goals, extending

their line of sight to include company needs and values, and sharing in the success of the enterprise. Variable pay, which is earned year by year and can take the form of cash and equity, can reward a combination of individual and collaborative results and focus on a host of financial and/or strategic measures and goals. Variable pay is not just for executives, managers and salespeople. It can be used as a key tool for the entire workforce. IBM and General Mills are among the many companies that reward all employees with variable pay for achieving results.

Spotlight on Incentives

Incentives are even more important in a quick-moving economy. While many companies have incentive programs, the results of these programs are starting to lag. Here are some tips to help power up your rewards:

- Put everyone on incentives or variable pay. Get the entire workforce in the performance results game. Everyone should be a stakeholder in company success. Build ownership from top to bottom so company success is broadly shared.
- Tie all incentives to business results. Make sure people understand how results make the enterprise succeed and grow. Cascade financial, customer, operational, people and future-focused goals. Avoid basing incentives on activities and duties, and show the workforce it is important to business outcomes.
- Use incentives for what people do best—emphasize measurable outcomes. Where possible, use shared goals that encourage collaboration and cooperation. Most enterprise successes result from people working together to accomplish critical success measures. Few individual goals can make an important business difference. Create a mentality of shared destiny—"We are in this together."
- Set stretch, yet achievable, goals. People must have a reasonable opportunity to earn awards. Missing unreasonably difficult goals destroys the power of incentives. Achieving stretch goals—but not slam-dunk goals—is a positive force for change and celebration.
- Select a few goals for incentives (three is best, but no more than five). Focus on the most important priorities—do not dilute the power of incentives. Many alternative goals exist. Choose the few that make the greatest performance difference. Often incentives that are provided deeply in an organization do not involve a large enough award to be divided among a lot of measures. It is better to achieve two or three key goals than to miss 10.
- Provide meaningful, upside opportunity for exceeding goals. Encourage people to go beyond goal achievement by increasing the award for exceeding goals.

- Calibrate incentives to ensure a win-win outcome for the organization and its people. Create a balance that allows the organization to gain in performance improvement and people to feel they receive a fair award for their effort.
- Keep communication and information levels high. Show progress toward goals and what is still needed in terms of performance. The primary role of incentives is to communicate, educate, involve, engage and create excitement—this requires company leaders to communicate continually. They must be out in front together, delivering the message of achievement.

The fast-moving economy is challenging, and it requires agility. New pay solutions are part of the response for smart companies. Total rewards are essential to making your company attractive to the best people and critical to getting everyone to make a performance difference. How do your pay solutions stack up? Is it time to "take the temperature" of the power and effectiveness of your enterprise's rewards?

First published in *Strategy & Leadership*, January/February 2001, 29 (1), 36-37.

Revisiting Effective Incentive Design: Still *The* Major ROI Reward Opportunity

W hy revisit basic incentive design anyway? Why use incentives? It is simple: to accelerate the performance of your organization and its people. When people can influence meeting goals and incentives are used as a part of employee pay, the organization's goals are much more likely to be achieved than when incentives are not used.

Research in many organizations shows well-designed incentives return about four times what the organization invests in incentive awards paid. For all incentive plans researched (good and not so good), the return on investment is double what is spent on incentives (WorldatWork's 1992 *Capitalizing on Human Assets*). Nothing else an organization can spend compensation dollars on can provide a similarly assured return on investment (ROI). So, even if you do not design and implement a "perfect" incentive plan the first time around, the returns are good for what you invest. But clearly it is more effective when it is designed right.

The Seven Principles of Incentive Design

The "secret sauce" of incentive design involves seven suggestions:

1. Know why incentives will help
2. Choose the right performance measures
3. Choose the right incentive design
4. Put the right amount of "stretch" in goals and measures
5. Measure performance where it counts the most
6. Evaluate outcomes and change as needed
7. Communicate, champion and don't give up.

If you follow these principles, you probably will add significant value to your organization. Whenever an incentive plan fails, the failure is commonly attributable to missing one or more of these key design principles.

Know Why Incentives Will Help

The *only* reasons to use incentives are to help improve performance and add value to the business. Using incentives must make it more likely that the organization will perform better. This reasoning is called a *business case* for an incentive plan. It justifies to CEOs the payoff for using incentives (i.e., ROI). It communicates the need for change to participants.

Some of the possible business reasons to consider incentives include:

- **Poor Performance.** Your organization's performance has become a "burning platform." The organization needs immediate significant change and major performance improvement to survive.
- **Marginally Acceptable Performance.** Performance in your organization has not gone dramatically awry, yet a course correction is needed. It is better to call people's attention to the need for change before a severe performance challenge exists.
- **Acceptable Performance.** Performance already may be good or even excellent, but the opportunity for an even better performance future exists.

The more pressing the business need that incentives help address, the easier it will be to justify and implement an incentive plan. Although, clearly, an organization must do much more than just implement an incentive plan to change culture; incentives help move from an entitlement mentality (where employees believe their performance does not affect their rewards) to a culture of rewarding results achieved.

What can you expect an incentive plan to do for your business and your employees? See Exhibit 5-1 for the 10 ways that incentives add value. The first principle is to build a solid business case. Organizations should state, in business terms, how an incentive plan adds value.

Choose the Right Performance Measures

Measures and goals are the metal from which the business case and value-added from incentives are forged. Incentives that provide a return on investment use measures and goals in one or more categories. (See Exhibit 5-2.)

Which measure your organization uses depends on what is most important and can be influenced by employees. Different functional and work groups, and types of employees, may influence different measures and goals. We use the word *influence* rather than *control*. Few employees, for instance, directly impact income or income growth. Many employees may influence these by impacting shorter-range financial goals, such as cost reduction or individual sales. Although people in constant contact with customers can directly impact customer service, many others can influence it.

Incentives can extend the employees' line-of-sight to goals they do not directly impact. This is accomplished by linking incentives to some intermediate goals and communicating to and educating employees on achieving the closer goals that ultimately influence the key but more remote goals.

Although some plans are more complex, a workable, understandable and accepted incentive plan usually has no more than three to five performance measures. This ensures that employees attend to and perform consistently with all the measures. Having too many measures is not only confusing but also permits employees to try to meet only some of the measures—often the easiest ones—because each measure counts less in the overall value of the incentive opportunity.

EXHIBIT 5-1 What Incentives Can Do

Objective #	Incentive Deliverable
1	Communicate—and focus people on—important organizational goals and directions.
2	Link people to measures of organizational performance.
3	Reward people for results achieved.
4	Develop a win-win partnership between people and the organization.
5	Vary pay with performance results.
6	Lead or reinforce other initiatives—customer value, continuous improvement, lean, quality, etc.
7	Extend people's line-of-sight to key measures and goals.
8	Stop paying an annuity for one year's performance.
9	Contain fixed pay costs.
10	Provide competitive total cash compensation.

EXHIBIT 5-2 Performance Measures and Categories

Category of Measure	Examples of Measures
Financial	Income and return ratios
Customer	Customer satisfaction, retention, penetration
Operational	Quality, cost, delivery, safety, efficiency
People	Retention, workforce satisfaction, results of development
Future-focused	New products, new services, breakthrough innovations, new markets

All incentive measures do not need to work the same way. In some cases, a measure can directly "fund" the incentive payment without concern for other measures. If success is achieved on this one measure, whether or not other goals are achieved makes no difference. The award on this measure is granted. Other incentive measures may serve as a "gate" to earn incentives based on another measure. For example, an insurance organization with customer service and quality incentives has a gate of a minimal level of financial performance that must be met to earn the full award achieved for the customer service and quality goals. The financial gate ensures the organization can afford the awards.

Other incentive goals "modify" the outcomes of funding goals. To use the manufacturing incentive example, it could be modified by goals of on-time delivery. When product is delivered as promised, the award for cost performance is modified upward. When commitments are missed, the award is modified downward and less incentive is granted. Measures also can be used to distribute incentive awards among incentive participants. For example, if overall company performance goals are met, a certain portion of the award is granted to certain divisions based on division performance. (See Exhibit 5-3.)

Measures and goals are at the core of incentive design. If an organization's measures do not make sense, it is impossible to have a viable incentive plan.

For example, a large retail grocery chain uses storewide incentives with the following four measures:

1. Customer satisfaction survey: Overall satisfaction of customers with the store.
2. Net sales compared to budget for the current period: Selling performance throughout the store.
3. Labor cost as a percentage of net sales compared to budget: Productivity of employees (including overtime) based on sales volume.

EXHIBIT 5-3 **How Certain Incentive Measures Work**	
Use of Incentive Measure	**How It Works**
Funders	Funds part of an award independent of funding other measures
Gate	Determines if any award based on performance on other measure(s) can be earned
Modifiers	Increases or decreases funding based on another measure
Distributors	Determines if funding based on other measure(s) is earned

4. Supplies cost as a percent of net sales compared to budget: the relative cost
    of supplies used in the store.

This chain focuses hourly employees in every store on a combination of customer satisfaction, sales and labor and supplies costs. A "gate" of store sanitation must be met before store employees are eligible to earn an award because store sanitation is so fundamental.

A chemical manufacturing plant focuses only on one measure: improvement in cost management. It shares 50 percent of cost per pound produced below the established budget with all employees in the manufacturing facility. There has been significant improvement in cost reduction because employees understand what impacts cost and are directly involved in managing cost effectively. The cost budget became the source of a win for the company and employees.

Choose the Right Incentive Design

Some incentive designs fit certain situations better than others. Organizations differ in structure and culture, as well as how they are organized (for example, some organizations are team based and others do not use teams). We selected four design alternatives, but in reality, organizations are most likely to take the best from a number of options and customize these to match their specific situation. The basic short-term incentive options are:

- **Business goal plan.** This design provides potential value added if applied on an organization, unit, department or team basis because it focuses on one or more of the key business metric areas. It is easiest to show value with an incentive plan that focuses on a key indicator of business success such as financial, customer, operational, people and future-focused goals. The value added to the organization at different levels of performance results helps set the incentive funding and incentive opportunity. When this results/reward relationship shows more value added to the organization than the incentive funding, the plan becomes self-funded (i.e., pays for itself).
- **Gainsharing plan.** This design focuses on cost savings, improvements in efficiency or increased productivity. Gainsharing plans share part of the savings with employees who help achieve the improvements. Eventually these plans can be so successful that it is very difficult to squeeze any more cost out of a specific organizational unit. At that time gainsharing plans may convert to goal plans.
- **Team incentive plan.** A business goal or gainsharing plan can focus on a small team. A team incentive plan shares the incentive earned from achieving goals

with team members. The focus is on shared goals—if one team member wins, the others do as well (the concept of shared destiny or "we are all in it together"). Support for the use of team incentives comes from research showing that teams using team-based incentives outperform those using only pay solutions based on individual team-member performance.

- **Individual incentive plans:** Where an employee's performance can be evaluated based on individual performance, organizations often create an individual incentive plan. An individual sales incentive plan based on personal sales is an example. Frequently, individual incentives are based on goal achievement that has a very close line-of-sight for the individual, so tying the individual to the larger organization's goals sometimes is a major challenge. Collaboration and cooperation are important in today's complex organizations. Sometimes care needs to be taken so employees who participate in individual incentives will help co-workers and not compete with others to the detriment of their combined effort.

Many possible incentive design combinations beg for customization. For example, one company decided its needs could be best served by combining an organizationwide incentive plan with a plan that focuses on individual performance. Having had experience with incentives, it was able to use more than the optimal three to five measures. The plan is complex and requires considerable communication. The goal balance is as follows:

- Organizationwide goals: weighted 70 percent
- Individual goals: weighted 30 percent

The organizationwide goal is to increase revenue, net profit, customer retention and customer penetration. Individual goals cascade from the organization's goals and relate to the employee's individual impact on organizational performance. The company believes that if individual employees have a combination of close line-of-sight individual incentive goals and longer line-of-sight organizational goals, they balance both cooperative and individual performance. (Another organization may have considered a team-based portion for the incentive design.)

Telephone customer service organizational units need to balance quality and productivity. A large service center uses a strong individual performance management and coaching system to focus on service quality and improve productivity. It implemented a team incentive based on the department team meeting or exceeding performance on four monthly team goals. This encouraged people to help each other and work together to reach common goals.

1. Decrease abandoned call rate for the month
2. Decrease telephone on-hold time
3. Increase quality as measured by audits
4. Increase call volume.

To qualify for an award, the participant must achieve individual quality and productivity goals. This solution creates a balance between quality and productivity and team and individual performance. The customer service organization is able to handle more calls at a high level of customer service and thus deliver great quality to more customers.

Many not-for-profit organizations use incentives below the executive level. For example, a medical group focuses on two goals that the board established: increased customer satisfaction and improved access to care. These two goals can be used throughout the organization for a wide range of people and units. The business case for these goals is that the organization has two things to sell: 1) customer satisfaction including high levels of clinical quality and a reputation for delivering outstanding care, and 2) patient access to this high-quality service in a timely manner and a productive delivery system that can keep its channels as a health-care provider filled.

Put the Right Amount of 'Stretch' in Goals and Measures

How is "excellent," "satisfactory" and "unsatisfactory" performance defined for incentive purposes? Typically, 80 percent of employees view their performance as "better than satisfactory" and the word "excellent" often has come to mean the minimum acceptable level of performance.

This raises the issue of setting goals that have enough "stretch" so they can be achieved and also provide a win for the organization and its employees. What is excellent performance as judged against a specific goal? What is the minimum level of goal achievement that justifies any incentive award at all? How do you make sure employees focus on performance goals throughout the entire performance period?

Exhibit 5-4 shows a number of ways to address the goal-setting process and suggests how to build stretch into goals.

Measure Performance Where It Counts the Most

Measure where the organization hopes to get optimum performance. Most organizations are interested in impacting organizationwide goals that represent a long line-of-sight to employees. However, to use these goals, organizations must make them "real" to

EXHIBIT 5-4 **Setting Stretch Performance Expectations**	
Basis for Setting Stretch Goals	**Description**
Business plan	If the business plan is reasonable and has stretch in it, then the incentive goals based on this plan also should be achievable but represent solid business performance.
Participation	People are more committed to achieving goals they help develop than goals that are developed for them. Getting input from participants in setting goals is valuable. But this does not mean the leadership team does not actually set the final performance goals and expectations.
Continuous improvement	Many organizations believe that if they set really tough goals, the workforce will figure out how to achieve them. But too-tough goals sometimes cause people to give up when they begin to miss early in the performance period. One antidote is to set realistic goals that have some improvement and increase the stretch in future performance periods. It is important to communicate upfront to employees that performance improvement will continue to be built into the goals.
World-class sustained	This means achieving a constant high-performance level that would be recognized as world-class performance. The organization is satisfied with consistent performance at this high level. This goal strategy often avoids needing to improve every year once great performance is achieved but requires consistency.
Compare to prior results	Many organizations set goal performance levels by exceeding the previous year's performance (ratcheting baselines). This ensures stretch goals but needs to be evaluated as a strategy because it may ignore the realities of the marketplace, customer needs or general economic conditions. Others may compare to the last couple of years to smooth out the performance expectations (rolling baselines).
Industry standards	How an organization compares to the performance of other organizations can provide an index of how the organization is doing from a comparative standpoint. Frequently outperforming competitors is a viable goal and takes into account factors that impact an industry uniformly.
Prevailing practice or "best" practice	What others do provides some organizations with clues about what they should do. There is considerable comfort in doing what others do, and this helps many organizations set goals and goal performance standards. However, what others do constitutes prevailing practice and not necessarily "best practice." What is "best" for one organization may also not be best for another and creates average performance. Comparing to best practice provides more of a stretch, depending on your organization's performance.

incentive participants. Considerable education and engaging employees in understanding how they impact these measures are necessary for organizationwide plans to be successful.

Organizational unit, team and department goals are medium line of sight. The challenge here is to link the individual to the organizational unit and the unit goals to the organization's goals. Team performance should also not be optimized at the expense of the organization.

Individual goals provide the closest employee line of sight but are more difficult to develop in a consistent quality manner across the organization. SMART (Specific, Measurable, Achievable, Realistic, Time-Sensitive) objectives or cascading goal methodology helps, but the challenge is to ensure all the individual goals add up to business value added to the organization and performance optimization across the organization.

Evaluate Outcomes and Change as Needed

When should or might you change incentive goals and for what reasons? A software development company set incentive goals based on expected improved performance over the prior year. The general economy turned down, making it impossible for the company to achieve its aggressive sales and profit goals and unlikely incentives would be paid. The CEO was concerned, feeling employees would give up because the goals he had believed were a reasonable stretch were actually not within reach. The conclusion was to adjust goals mid-year to more reasonable expectations and strongly communicate the need to help the organization get through the year. In this instance, it worked. In other companies, adjusting goals may not have been affordable.

Typically, organizations consider changing goals or performance requirements relative to measures at the start of the next performance period. It is important at this time to match measures and goals to the organization's business plan and the realities of the marketplace. This also gives the organization a significant communication opportunity to let the incentive participants know what is expected and how they fit in.

The real question is about changing goals and goal requirements midstream. Some of the business reasons organizations may find compelling enough to warrant changing performance expectations and incentive goals during the middle of a performance period could include the following:

- Changes in business strategy/plan objectives that cannot wait for the start of a new performance period
- Capital or technology changes that happen during a performance period
- Product mix changes

- Competitive necessity or improvements
- Accounting changes.

The key issue is the immediate nature of the need to change. It makes no sense to stay the course when the situation changes significantly and dramatically, and incentive goals will serve only to undermine new directions and priorities.

Communicate and Champion

Implementing incentives where none exist is a "hot" change. Changing from a base pay-only program to incentives gets everyone's attention and gets it quickly. And it is "noisy" change that may create concern.

So it is essential to tell why you are changing rewards and adding incentives. What is the present situation relative to the organization and workforce? Why must the situation change? What desired future state is the organization seeking as a result of adding incentives? Where do people fit in the formula for change? How will their pay be influenced and what must they do to receive an incentive award?

One new CEO decided the reason for incentives was to change the workforce's strong focus on an entitlement mentality. The CEO implemented incentives to send a message that adding value to the organization is critical to organizational success. It put some "skin in the game" so employees became interested in how the organization performed on key incentive goals.

The main cause of incentive failure is lack of championing and sponsorship from the top of the organization. Senior leadership must educate on the importance of goal achievement. Championing must be continuous, not just at the start of the incentive plan. Incentives are the responsibility of the managers from top to bottom—helping to set goals, coaching employees on how to reach the goals, problem solving with employees, removing barriers to performance, communicating and helping explain and ensure everyone knows what is required of them. The reason for the incentive is improved results, and the incentive plan serves as a communication vehicle to accomplish this.

We like to get employees involved in helping to design the incentive plan. Whether they are part of a focus group or on an actual design team depends on the organization and the situation. But involving people who will actually be incentive participants in the design of the plan is invaluable. They are able to provide inputs and improvements. Their most important and powerful role, however, is in their communication and support of the plan. They can begin the communication process at the start of the design and be involved throughout the life of the plan. And they play an important role when the plan is evaluated—at least annually.

Don't Give Up!

Implementing an incentive plan represents a major change. Most employees are used to getting a fixed paycheck, and many have never had any of their compensation depend directly on their performance. A "merit" increase is most often diluted with issues of internal equity, competitiveness, cost of living, promotions, and the like, meaning little of it is really for merit at all. Incentives for performance are a big change, and the organization's leaders must be ready to stick with the change process for several years at least.

If your CEO asks, "What's the biggest bang-for-the-buck change we can make in compensation in the next year?", incentives may be the answer. It may be time to look at these seven incentive design principles.

Incentives work, and most organizations need them somewhere right now. Incentives provide a great opportunity for pay and rewards professionals to "put some performance bread on the company's table" this year and next. Many organizations are working through the challenges and opportunities that incentives present and are getting added value now.

First published in *WorldatWork Journal*, First Quarter 2005, 14 (1), 50-58.

CHAPTER 6:

Best-Practice Incentives for Contact Centers and Distribution Centers: Driving Customer Satisfaction

Most companies selling products or services to customers have a contact center (customer service or inbound call center), and product-based companies have a distribution center. The performance of employees in both of these centers dramatically influences their company's performance in the eyes of their customers. Customer service representatives (CSRs) are in daily contact with customers; material handlers (distribution center employees) are the last employees to touch products before they reach customers.

Most CEOs and HR leaders indicate both of these centers substantially impact key metrics such as customer satisfaction, overall sales, sales per order, cost of service and returns. Performance improvements in customer service and distribution influence bottom-line performance and serve as a leading-edge move to real pay for performance throughout the company. As one CEO said, "It does little good to have market-making products if your customers are ill served and you can't deliver what they buy in an effective fashion."

The focus of this chapter is achieving and sustaining strong performance in these two organizational units by linking the performance results of employees in these centers with compensation—specifically incentives. A sample of large technology-based manufacturing companies that provide incentives to CSRs, material handlers and their supervisors was surveyed to determine best practices and lessons learned so survey results could help other companies get the most value from their incentives more quickly. Companies selected had reputations for high-quality customer service and on-time and high-quality delivery of manufactured products. These companies are viewed as practice leaders in numerous progressive HR programs that reflect true pay-for-performance attributes. These survey results are also consistent with Schuster-Zingheim and Associates' knowledge of incentives in some of the most benchmarked companies commonly viewed as high performance, and with the authors' considerable experience designing incentives. The concept for this study grew out of our article, "Linking Quality and Pay."

Incentive Principles

Surveyed companies base their incentives for contact centers and distribution centers on the following principles (as summarized in Exhibit 6-1):

- **Agility in reward design:** The companies remain willing to change any element of these incentive plans to respond to the customer, market, economics or strategy, or just because that element is not getting the job done. Compensation solutions must be aligned with business realities.

- **Extension of the business:** Incentives are viewed as business tools that communicate values and directions to specific workforces about goals and priorities these workforces can influence. Incentive design comes from a business case for change, and employees understand the role incentives play in the business process.

- **Creation of customer partnerships:** Incentives are designed to make allies of employees and customers. Incentives do not reward performance from employees who are making decisions that are not in the customers' interests.

- **Few metrics and frequent awards.** These incentive plans use two to four metrics or goals consistent with the concept that everything worth working on and measuring does not belong in an incentive plan. Only those most important metrics are used for incentives. Too many metrics lose focus and may result in people working on easier, achievable, but less critical goals than the key stretch goals that drive the business. And the companies measure performance and grant awards frequently. The companies also give feedback, coach and make course corrections concurrently.

- **Awards "de-linked" from base pay:** Incentive payments are not granted as a percentage of base pay. Rather they are the same-size awards for the same performance level without regard to an employee's base pay.

- **Transparency to customers and employees:** Customers visit the work site of these employees. The incentive plan is a selling point to show customers that employees are paid for satisfying the customers. Customers see posted incentive

EXHIBIT 6-1 **Incentive Principles**	
1. Agility in reward design	5. Awards "de-linked" from base pay
2. Extension of the business	6. Transparency to customers and employees
3. Creation of customer partnerships	
4. Few metrics and frequent rewards	

metrics and are asked to give feedback about the incentive plan metrics, often in the presence of employees.

These companies do not focus on how employees in one segment of the organization are paid compared to how employees in another are paid. Internal equity across organizational units is not a focus in the decision process for incentive design.

Incentive Design

These companies start their incentive design process by finding out how customers measure the value that CSRs and material handlers add to the customers' experience. This information is used to build incentive metrics that are viewed as opportunities to partner with customers. This means avoiding nearly all metrics involving sales, cost, profitability, specific product or service emphases and metrics influencing buying or delivery preferences. Exhibit 6-2 compares contact and distribution center incentives.

Unit of Measurement

In the same company, the unit of measurement for incentives typically differs between contact centers and distribution centers because the unit of measurement is based on the center's business case.

Customer service in contact centers is viewed as dependent on the performance of an individual because individuals interface with customers and are responsible for managing the immediate relationship, considered the "make-or-break" time. One participant said, "We use small teams to problem-solve customer service but not to reward performance. It is the individual who translates what they know into

EXHIBIT 6-2 **Comparison of Contact and Distribution Center Incentives**		
Element	Contact Center	Distribution Center
Objective	Seamless customer service	On-time delivery
Work element	Each contact: phone call, e-mail	Order receipt/logged in; process performed; out the door or customer receipt
Unit for incentive award	Individual performance primarily	Distribution centerwide performance
Eligibility	Individual	Individual
Performance period	Every two weeks, monthly or weekly	Weekly or every two weeks

performance to earn the reward." So contact center incentives are designed for individual performance. Companies believe before considering team incentives that it is critical to have small teams and ensure the work is done in small teams.

Distribution is different because the performance the customer "feels" is influenced directly from the point when the order is logged into the organization to when the order is received by the customer. This is measuring performance end-to-end in the context of distribution workforces. Success in a distribution center can be measured at points between logging in the order and customer delivery. However, excellent performance mid-stream is unimportant to the customer. Only receiving the correct order when promised counts. Small teams may exist and individual performance is important, but excellent-performing small teams and individuals cannot make up for the distribution center's inability to deliver on promises.

The companies use performance management for individual performance in distribution centers. Individual performance focuses on what each employee can do to make the distribution center successful. Where teams exist, some use a multi-rater system that comprises the incremental delivery from one station to the next. However, only centerwide incentives are used with a "we are all in this together" focus because performance is measured end-to-end in a distribution center. This solution lets everyone know how the distribution center is doing so they can mutually help improve performance. Distribution centerwide incentives communicate that the center cannot have pockets of differences in performance levels and deliver effectively to the customer.

Metrics

Using few incentive metrics was consistently considered better than using many. "Experience suggests that two or three metrics can easily cover the entire message we want to give to employees about serving customer needs," one participant said. The view generally is that once a metric is worth less than one-third or one-fourth of the total incentive value, it does not get enough employee attention. "Many important things don't need to be measured for incentive determination purposes" was the position these organizations take. All reported they had to resist senior management's tendency to expect the incentive plan to manage the people and not have supervisors do it.

Contact Center Metrics. These practices come from business goals and should be best practice only if an organization has the same business goals as the benchmark companies. Metrics for CSRs, who spend most of their time on the phone, are in order of frequency of use by companies:

- Speed of answering calls (X percent of calls answered within Y seconds)
- Dropped calls as percent of total calls
- Percent call time or call time as a percentage of time available on the phone
- Call volume (e.g., number of calls answered compared to available time, number of orders logged and confirmed)
- Customer satisfaction based on after-call customer input
- Average call time or average call-handle time.

No surveyed organization used internal measurement of call quality (e.g., using a call-monitoring system) as an incentive metric because it is viewed as either excessively subjective or part of a proactive coaching, training and performance management process. Call quality is, however, important to the customer interaction and therefore to these companies, so they use call monitoring for performance improvement feedback and coaching, but not for incentive award purposes. None use secret shoppers making test calls to evaluate CSR performance. They use only objective incentive metrics and show CSRs how they work before associating them with pay awards of any kind. Internal measurement of quality using a call-monitoring system and evaluating CSRs on, for example, providing accurate information, listening, asking the right questions to solve the problem and voice quality likely correlates with, but is a different metric from, customer satisfaction that is immediately measured after the CSR hangs up but before the customer hangs up.

The uniform objective from an organizational standpoint is to complete as many calls as possible with the customers going away well-satisfied and looking forward to their next encounter with contact-center staff. To do this, CSRs often are trained to listen to customers 80 percent of the time and talk 20 percent of the time.

Distribution Metrics. The companies did not design distribution incentives with a financial focus to maximize productivity but rather to make material handlers partners with the customers. Companies used two to four distribution incentive metrics. In order of frequency, the incentive metrics include the following:

- Timeliness of shipment to customer
- Accuracy of orders
- Volume of orders shipped
- Cycle time from order receipt to shipping
- Customer complaints or returns
- Safety.

Organizations do not differentiate by shift or area, so difficult work is not left or transferred to another. Only one company has different metrics and performance levels for "pickers" and "packers." Engineered standards are avoided to prevent gaming between employees and engineers at the expense of the company and customers.

Goal Setting

To keep the incentive "un-entitled" and agile, surveyed companies change metrics, goals and performance levels when needed (usually annually) to give more communication opportunities and to ensure continuous improvement. Several issues may initiate changes to metrics and goals, such as continuous improvement, business need or changes in processes, technology, equipment, work flow, staffing, customer expectations and business direction. Companies discuss changes with the workforce before the change and typically give 60- to 90-days' notice. Companies believe making the metrics current and fluid to business needs is important.

Examples of changes in equipment that would result in re-evaluation of incentive goals in contact centers are upgrading the flow of computer screens for easier information access that would result in shorter phone calls, and improved scheduling from a new workforce-management system that would result in a faster average speed of answering calls. A distribution center that converts to radio frequency equipment (automated reading of bar codes) would likely increase accuracy and productivity goals after employees are trained and have become accustomed to the new technology. Distribution centers often scale incentive performance levels and base the threshold level on a percent of prior performance—for example, same time frame—provided the business has not had one of the changes that result in a modification of metrics or goals.

Award Frequency

"Can we grant awards daily?" was the question one CEO posed to company management and the HR team. None of the surveyed companies has performance periods longer than monthly, and most are biweekly or weekly because frequency is important. The more frequent the recognition, the better employees and the companies like it. For companies, it is not the issue of providing cash flow to employees—rather it is having frequent opportunities to give feedback and make course corrections in the performance management process. Each time the workforce receives awards, the supervisor discusses the reasons for the award, what it means and what is on the horizon to sustain or improve during the next performance period. The goal is continuous improvement and setting a course for success. The more often this can happen, the organizations believe, the better.

Award Size

Median and average awards for the surveyed companies range from 9 percent to 13 percent of the average base pay of a company's participants in these incentives. Survey participants said that the amount is less important than the message the awards deliver. And most of these companies grant awards based on equal-dollar amounts, not as a percent of base pay, to put a clear dollar value on achieving the metric.

This means that highest-paid and lowest-paid workforce members receive the same dollar award for achieving a specific goal level. "Meeting the goal requirements is what counts—not how much you are paid in base pay," one participant said. Goals are not worth more or less, depending on the employee's base pay. The companies feel a sense of "team" on an overall basis is better achieved if awards fit the performance and not the base pay level. Regardless of the form of incentive award, companies must comply with the Fair Labor Standards Act (FLSA) about overtime payments for incentive plans with prospective goals for nonexempt employees.

Incentive awards are part of a communication and recognition strategy. The surveyed companies do not believe they would get more value from significantly larger awards. The message and communications are what they are after.

Communication

One survey participant said, "Communication is everything." These incentives give organizations the opportunity to communicate important goals and engage the workforce in influencing these goals. Frequent discussion permits extending employees' line of sight to the broader business impact of their work and broader business goals and results.

No surveyed company discussed "motivating" with incentives; they discussed communicating the company's expectations and having employees decide whether or not they are on board. "Pay encourages and reinforces what the company wants as part of the win-win, and the employee takes it from there. Also it states what it is about working here from the start—no false expectations are created," one survey participant said.

Engagement is an integral part of the process. Employees have the opportunity to discuss organizational performance results, problem solve and give feedback. Most companies involved employees in plan design and asked them to help monitor the plan for effectiveness on a continuing basis.

Integration with Other Reward Components

These incentives are part of an overall rewards strategy. Both types of centers use frequent recognition (tangible, symbolic and verbal/written) and celebration, with the focus depending on the type of center and the company's specific business objectives. Both often recognize employees for customer praise, suggestions and specific metrics of immediate importance, while contact centers often recognize individual volumes, and distribution centers often recognize safety.

Contact centers also may use a career level or skill program for base pay. This provides career levels that are based on proficiency in additional content areas and corresponding pay increases for using additional skills. The business objectives are: (1) customers being served in one phone call rather than being transferred and (2) retaining employees longer than typical in contact-center jobs so the company receives a return on its training investment. CSRs win with career and base pay progression as they add value. Companies may also provide CSRs with flexible scheduling, a work-life benefit, provided the scheduling fits customer flow and the individual continues to meet performance requirements.

Supervisors

Supervisors are eligible for the center incentive, so they are advocates of the incentive and their goals are aligned with the employees they supervise. Incentive goals that are important to customer service make business sense not only for nonexempt or hourly employees but also for their supervisors so "everyone is on the same page." Contact-center supervisors typically have goals reflecting the overall performance of the CSRs reporting to them. Distribution supervisors have either the same plan as their employees, the same plan but with a few additional metrics such as cost management or another plan including the material handlers' incentive metrics.

Supervisors are viewed as very important, not for their technical knowledge as much as for their willingness and ability to coach, provide feedback and train. They must be leaders at communicating and getting employees to understand their role in the context of the business and the customers. Supervisors understand the metrics and use the incentive plan and the distribution of incentive checks as a teaching and coaching tool. They communicate progress about goals and engage the workforce in making suggestions and improving processes. It means hiring, training and developing supervisors who are coaches, trainers and communicators, not "bosses." Promoting leads with demonstrated coaching and communication skills facilitates having supervisors who are not only technically strong but also have supervisory capabilities.

Conclusion

Contact centers and distribution centers are important to the business, so these companies ensure that incentive plans acknowledge this reality. During a time when many companies are designing incentives based on metrics that reward increasing profit, sales and other quantitative metrics of ROI improvement, these companies are aligning themselves with customers. They believe this win-win will help the bottom line of their company and of their customers.

Rewards design is becoming a tool geared to accelerating the business process, as these companies have shown. A key learning is the rewards customization process within the company to fit each center's business needs. The practices summarized in this chapter may be a place to start your company's rewards customization process based on its business needs.

First published in *WorldatWork Journal*, Third Quarter 2006, 15 (3), 32-38.

PART III
Adding Value through Base Pay

CHAPTER 7:

Can Base Pay Reward Performance?

Base pay is the largest single element of HR cost. Getting the most out of expenditures on base pay is or should be a priority. Most organizations state in their HR policy manual or employee handbook that they pay for performance, but do they really? Can base pay be used to pay for performance?

Major surveys suggest many organizations have lost confidence in traditional "merit" increase plans. This is because scarce base pay adjustment dollars have so many demands on them—responding to competitive practice, reflecting the value of work performed, paying for geographic differentials, rewarding tenure and a host of other purposes, leaving little money or opportunity to reward skill, competence or performance. Often organizations feel not enough dollars remain to recognize differences in performance so they make only meager attempts to do so.

Double-Barreled Solution

One way organizations focus on paying for performance is through the broadening use of variable pay and incentives. Incentives do not fold into base pay and must be re-earned each performance period. Eighty percent of companies use some form of variable pay or incentives below the supervisory or management level. Variable pay has become the "tool of choice" for rewarding employee performance. Not only does variable pay reduce the risk of becoming either an entitlement or a "gift that keeps on giving" for one good year of performance, incentives are also agile, flexible, able to be customized to match a host of changing and evolving organizational needs, and actually work.

It seems apparent to us that no matter how effective adjustments to base pay may become for rewarding performance, incentives and variable pay will be the premier way to reward performance. If base pay can be made to be more responsive to performance, it is possible that pay for performance can be addressed with a "double-barreled" solution. Here is how base pay and incentives may be combined to support creating a performance culture:

- **Base pay adjustments:** Ties the largest element of cash compensation, base pay, to performance differences. The eventual goal is to pay the employees with the most critical skills and competencies for translating this capability into strong performance or value added to the business over time. Because base pay is seldom successfully cut or reduced, the priority is to design a base pay system that pays more to top performers with critical skills and competencies over time. Sustained performance over time is something base pay can recognize, but getting from where base pay is now to this solution requires change.

- **Incentives and variable pay:** Reward short and long-term results. Link the employee as an individual or as a member of an organizational unit, team, function, or company to business goals and customer success measures. Evidence and experience suggest that the best compensation ROI comes from a straightforward incentive plan for all employees throughout an organization or organizational unit.

The combination of the two elements is a potentially powerful one that communicates a performance culture. Clearly showing that performance matters from the start is the best way to combat the creation of an entitlement mentality.

If there is a "problem" with incentives, it is that no matter how large the incentive opportunity is, it is smaller than the base pay employees are paid (exceptions are some sales professionals and executives). And it may even be less than the base pay adjustment budget managers have to distribute annually. If the major component of pay is based on something other than differences in skills, competencies, and performance, employees understand that non-performance elements are more important pay determiners than are those related to performance differences.

Why Repair 'Merit Pay'?

High-performance organizations attract talented people who want their performance rewarded. The top 20 percent of performers often generate about 80 percent of the results achieved by an organization. However, base pay is universally more likely to be correlated with length of service and years of experience than differences in employee performance by any measure. This often makes it difficult to communicate to a workforce that performance is rewarded. It is nearly impossible to build credibility in a communication message about paying for performance if it is not consistent with practice.

How many believers in paying for performance do you think a CEO will get if the message to communicate is, "I know our company pays mostly for years of service and experience and not performance. However, believe what I say and not what I do—paying for performance is the way we wish it were." Fixing how raises are granted is important but difficult to do. Improvements can be made to clarify the message about the value of adding value to the business.

Improving Base Pay for Performance

First, stop what you are doing relative to granting base pay adjustments. Although this may be like turning a ship headed for an iceberg, it is essential and gives the message that a course correction is in the making. Trying to "fine tune" an annual budget number in order that monies presently deployed for everything from competitive practices to recognizing performance has proven to be unreasonable. There is little evidence of success by merely attempting to re-arrange the deck chairs on the sinking merit-pay Titanic. You can certainly try to do this, but it is difficult to communicate change when the workforce is seeing minor versions of the same old solutions and not a significant difference.

Meaningful change must start with visible change so people do not say, "This too will pass." Introduce different ways to use base pay and base pay adjustments to help incentive plans pay for performance. Create a new learning platform for pay management so the rules change and the communications surrounding how people are paid and what they are paid for change as well. Put strategic intent into the largest expense many organizations have—what they spend on base pay. Do not just hook on some technology gimmick that helps manage pay better but improve the foundation so it magnifies organizational goal performance.

Most attempts to make merit pay work fail because they are generally based on admonitions to "try harder" or "make the existing solutions work" or "train people better." All of this is good advice and should be considered. However, it seldom seems to work. Jawboning supervisors and managers is an important way to improve how they pay for performance. The problem is keeping at it. Because so many initiatives come and go that employees are often dizzy, organizations tend to go back to the way it was before with a "this too will pass" view of a new initiative because "we know another new one is just around the corner."

Suggestions for Changing Base Pay Increases

A base pay increase stays with people throughout their entire career with the organization, no matter how their value changes. It is nearly impossible to reduce base pay to match performance and retain someone in the organization—unless, of course, they cannot find work elsewhere because they remain overpaid for the value they add or because they are just putting in their time to retirement. Anything you can do to align base pay with performance is heavy lifting, but if you can do it, this better aligns a huge opportunity cost with performance and value to the business. Here are eight action steps to help paying for performance greatly:

Action Step No. 1: Improve the performance management foundation. Involve the organization in evaluating and improving the current performance management process. Cascade goals throughout the organization, engage people in their own performance management process, focus on adding business value and growth/improvement, emphasize ongoing feedback and coaching, and gain consensus on the calibration of the "performance bar."

Action Step No. 2: Do not allocate base pay budget equally to all organizational units or departments. Instead, allocate the increase budget with preference for organizational areas that have demonstrated high performance and excellent results or to those areas with critical skills and competencies essential to business goals and objectives. Alternatively allocate more base pay increase dollars to areas where the competitive labor market has moved the most and where more money is needed to remain competitive with the specific market in which the organization competes for talent.

Action Step No. 3: Include more than just the individual's immediate manager in determining base pay increases. Often managers alone do not do a good job of allocating base pay increases. A group of managers working together with its senior manager can determine increases using employee performance evaluations as the basis for the adjustments. This also helps improve goal setting and calibration of performance levels and helps move to more uniform solutions that make it more probable that similar results will receive similar pay treatment. Smaller companies can centralize base pay increase decisions based on performance evaluations and manager inputs. Creating shared responsibility for the allocation of base pay increases improves objectivity and accountability.

Action Step No. 4: Have managers rank people based on sustained value-added, contributions, results achieved and other performance elements. Then compare the ranking to current base pay to see what changes need to be made over time for greater alignment. The goal is to repair this inequity and redefine fairness in terms of value to the business. The objective over time is to pay the best performers more than competitive levels of base pay to make performance worthwhile and to reward people based on their track record of performance over time.

Action Step No. 5: Think in terms of resulting base pay (absolute dollars). Do not focus on percent increases that sustain existing inequities in base pay. Using absolute annual base pay dollars stops magnifying base pay inequities and permits lower-paid, better performers to catch up with higher-paid employees whose performance may not justify their existing pay. An equal-dollar award of, for example, $2,000 represents a larger percent for a lower-paid employee than a higher-paid employee who may be adding equal value to the organization.

Action Step No. 6: Focus more on the results achieved than on behaviors. Results are the way businesses measure value added and what makes businesses successful. Use the performance management process to coach people on behaviors to improve measurable results. Weight behaviors less than results. Alternatively, do not have behaviors impact pay unless they are negative enough to get in the way of results. For example, determination of goal achievement considers not only what was accomplished but how it was accomplished—particularly if behaviors were inconsistent with the organization's values. Use recognition to reward behaviors. There are too few base pay increase dollars available to focus them on rewarding behaviors. Focus only on an individual's sustained value added to the organization over time.

Action Step No. 7: Give priority to differentiating the pay of top performers from everyone else. Do what it takes to pay a premium for the high performers. Earmark a small part of the total salary increase budget to use only to enhance the increases of the high performers. Alternatively, as a supplement to base pay increases for high performers, implement a variable pay or lump-sum payment, for example, based on outstanding business results and make the awarding of this reward visible. Or if the initial pass on base pay increases overspends the budget, balance the budget by reducing increases to lower or typical performers rather than all employees or the top performers. Make performance excellence worthwhile.

Action Step No. 8: Know the competitive labor market and consider it when making performance base pay decisions. Reserve most base pay adjustments for the top performers so increases are significant—especially those paid below the competitive labor market with a track record of sustained high performance over time. Employees with high base pay relative to their job's labor market worth need to be a top performer to receive a pay increase or a variable pay award. Consider lump-sum payments instead of a base pay increase for higher-paid employees compared to the labor market. Look for ways other than increasing base pay to reward excellent performance over a short term for highly paid employees. The short-term performance may not be sustained and the result may be an employee paid more than their overall value to the business over time. The unfair and unjust approach is to let someone's base pay grow until they are overpaid late in life and in their career. It is better to be honest early in people's careers rather than avoid telling them the truth and letting them be paid more than they are worth and then having them feel trapped at an organization or having the organization lay them off.

The Future

Using base pay for rewarding performance is important because of the message it sends about the largest element in the total pay equation. We have suggested alternatives to consider that go beyond trying to get managers to "do better" with the existing methodologies. Some involve substantial change from what is done now and when combined with variable pay can help organizations gain more value from their base pay adjustment dollars.

Reprinted from www.hr.com, September-October 2006.

CHAPTER 8:
Measuring the Value of Work

P eople, not jobs, provide advantage to organizations. When was the last time you saw a job handle customers effectively, invent a product or service, or even operate a computer? Employees acquire and apply the skill and competence businesses need. All talent strategies focus on the need to hire great people and create a high-performance workplace that enables them to perform well. These strategies count on people to grow throughout their careers by acquiring and applying essential capabilities so they increase their value over time. Everything is focused on people and how they work—little is said about jobs. Why do organizations continue to pay for jobs and not the people with the skills and competencies who occupy those jobs?

Perhaps the reason lies in the momentum of habit and the lack of a practical way to pay for skill and competence. However, through the Internet, some organizations are presently innovating Web-based pay systems, which may be the "secret sauce" that could make paying directly for skill and competency finally attainable.

While admitting that first-generation skill and competency pay solutions were problematic, many reasons for failure can be addressed by piecing together solutions that now exist. By focusing on simplicity, Internet-based solutions can be successful. This means discarding the overdesigned and complicated skill-pay systems of the past. This article explores the means and methods to developing a people-based pay system. But the first step in the process of improvement is learning from past mistakes.

The Reasons for 'Job' Valuation

What is the state of the art in determining the value of work? "Jobs" are ways to organize and classify the work an organization needs completed. There is a long history of how jobs and the people who hold them are valued. For many years the point-factor methodologies were dominant in setting salary levels and external and internal job values. This was without doubt the most influential compensation tool used by organizations of all sizes and types, from the 1940s through the 1980s. This method still dominates job valuing, especially in Europe and developing countries. The most pervasive of this class of job-valuing tools is the Hay plan.

However, while extremely popular, the point-factor method failed to evolve and adapt as organizational needs changed. The internal value of jobs needed to be better correlated with the competitive value of jobs and the pay necessary to hire and retain quality talent. The strong focus of point-factor plans on internal equity created multiple challenges for user organizations. Jobs of similar perceived internal worth to an organization often had completely different market values. The result of this in some instances was for the organization to overpay employees in jobs that were internally valued the same as jobs with high market value. And the reverse was more problematic because it sometimes created a situation where jobs were underpaid when they had the same internal value as jobs with lower market value. A situation could exist where organizations were not paying incumbents competitively in the most market-sensitive jobs.

The Move to Market Pricing

Even before the time of freely available survey information on the Web, the competitive market became at least as important as perceived internal value. Organizations were focusing less on retaining "career" workers and more on short-term employees. Employees spent their working lives with several organizations rather than just one, so what other organizations paid became more important than what just the employer paid internally. In addition, point-factor plans and other job-valuing plans were laborious and time-consuming to manage. Because the vendors of point-factor plans were unable to simplify them and because the compensable elements were often not strongly correlated with the external market, these plans lost credibility in organizations more focused on external competitiveness.

Organizations adopted the market ranking of jobs, which amounts to comparing the described jobs to survey job descriptions and placing them in ranges or assigning market reference values that approximated competitive practice. Subsequently, jobs for which direct market information was not available would be ranked compared to the market-placed benchmark jobs. The benchmark jobs for which competitive survey data are available anchor the placement of jobs for which survey data are not available. And the entire ranked solution results in the jobs with the highest market value placed in salary ranges or salary bands near the top of the pay system and other jobs placed respectively lower in the overall picture. Jobs with the greatest market value are placed in order so that incumbents of these jobs are eligible for the highest pay. And other jobs are ranked accordingly.

Some Organizations Need More Verification

The market-ranking process has proven to be sound and solidifies the fact that the realities of the external marketplace are the most important determiner of job value. However, job value should be modified in accordance with the strategic value to the organization, the skills and competencies needed to perform the job and the relative scarcity of talent to fill specific roles in the organization. This solution also turns out to be less bureaucratic and burdensome than does the use of formal point-factor programs. The reality is that organizations are no longer able to field a deep cadre of professionals to manage a complex job-valuing system. However, market ranking is a judgment call in many instances and does not provide for a careful analysis of the job elements.

Organizations often find it difficult to explain market ranking as a job-valuing solution. There are several reasons for this:

• Organizations hoping to focus more on the critical skills and competencies employees possess rather than on the jobs to which they are assigned may be uncertain about how the worth of competencies and skills relates to job worth.

• Job matching with survey benchmarks is viewed as subjective and as much an "art form" as a "science."

• Placement of jobs for which data are not directly available may seem as much an "estimate" as matching based on responsibilities, skills and competencies.

• Often confusion exists about how internal job value is rationalized with the market value of jobs.

• The popularity of broadbanding and career-progression systems is often hard to integrate with market valuing.

Other issues suggest that alternatives to basic market ranking are needed. However, the future of job valuing does not lie in a return to internal job valuing such as that represented in point-factor plans, which give preference to internal equity over market valuing.

The Status of Job-Valuing Today

During the last decade, point-factor plans were commonly modified to match the realities of the competitive marketplace. The process of first establishing the relative internal value of all jobs and then trying to fit the results to the market was not working. Instead dislocations from the market were creating untenable pay programs—overpaying some jobs and underpaying others. Once the organization had established a total internal structure for job valuing from top to bottom, it was hard to reconcile the total result with the market. For example, assume that the total point value for jobs ranges from a high of 10,000 value points to a low of 1,000 value points. Sometimes two jobs with an internal worth of around 2,000 value points have dramatically different market values. Although the knowledge, skills and responsibilities may differ, the total point accumulation suggests the same salary range or band placement.

One of the first techniques used to fix these plans so that they reconcile the market and internal value was to score all jobs without preweighting the elements of job value, factors such as knowledge requirements; indicators of job scope, responsibility and management; and asset accountabilities. After job scoring was performed, the elements of job value were weighted using multiple-regression analysis so that those elements that best explained external market value could be weighted more than the elements that were less proficient in explaining market values. Elements of job value that are the best predictors of the market, such as organizational level and management responsibilities, would get more weight than those weaker in explaining external market value. As a result, total scores of jobs would be strongly predictive of the external market, so the organization was addressing both internal and external job value.

The value systems relative to jobs, skills and competencies have changed dramatically over the years. Compensable factors that pay the most for managing people and other resources create problems for organizations. First, being a manager is not necessarily the most valuable responsibility in all organizations. Many organizations want career ladders that encourage growth along nonmanagement routes as well. Valuing management encourages competition to manage resources, creating levels and layers in the organization that may not be needed. It also encourages people who are excellent individual and team contributors in nonmanagement roles to seek management roles because these jobs pay more, forcing a move to a work role that people may not be qualified to perform. So, the actual compensable elements need to be brought up-to-date to better match the realities of work and organizational priorities.

New Solutions

Experience trying to make canned job-valuing solutions work, combined with the realities of the competitive marketplace for talent, have suggested that there is possibly a better way to address job valuing that combines the elements we know best predict market and also represent the realities for organizations now and in the future. How will organizations create a job-valuing system that is agile and flexible enough to remain current through continuous improvement?

The two features of job valuing that will ensure future progression include:

- Compensable elements that reflect contemporary organization designs and also correlate with job value in the market
- Market data that can be used to correlate the value of the compensable elements with what they are worth in the competitive marketplace.

Although these have existed in job valuing before, the issues of market and contemporary job worth have not been addressed until recently. The external market in contemporary times is the best way to determine the value of skills and talent. The objective is to identify the compensable elements that best predict the relative market for skills and talent in the external marketplace.

Compensable Elements

What makes skills, competencies, the role the employee plays in the organization or "the job itself" more or less valuable? Organizations and various governmental agencies remain concerned about the potential discriminatory nature of any tools or yardsticks organizations use to determine the value of work in monetary terms. Because of this, many believe the best way to address the issue of paying fairly is to base how employees are paid upon accurate descriptions of skills, competencies, and work and job content, but then also to identify the features and characteristics about these that most correlate with how the market determines what is most valuable about people who perform work.

Research suggests that the compensable elements most often used to determine the value of work to an organization vary widely in their ability to predict the market value of work performed. For instance, jobs that are responsible for the management of people and assets are normally more valuable than those without such accountabilities. However, one of the most important determiners of the market worth of a job is the functional area in which the work is performed: accounting, computer systems, sales management, quality control, etc. Yet these factors are seldom part of any job-valuing tools. Also, the type of people supervised—scientists, engineers, actuaries, manufacturing assemblers, clerical support, lawyers, etc.—is important in determining what the market pays for management jobs.

Accountability has not typically been defined in terms that give work roles without management accountability strong value. However, because of the changes in how organizations are designed and the premium placed on unique skills and core competencies that may not involve supervision or management of people or assets—but rather the development, creation and commercialization of ideas—many nonmanagement skills and competencies equal or surpass the market value of traditional supervision and management responsibilities. The challenge is then to select the compensable elements that define contemporary work in modern organizations and use these as the foundation of determining the worth of work.

Years of repairing job-valuing solutions in order to credibly match the way modern work is performed and valued has generated a list of some compensable elements that represent work and how it is valued internally and externally in the marketplace. There are several key compensable elements:

- Functional area (e.g., HR, finance, accounting)
- Specific technical expertise
- Level of technical expertise
- Learning and experience equivalents
- Leadership accountability, including team leadership
- Innovation, complexity, creativity
- Language skills—reading, verbal and written communications
- Mathematical and statistical skills
- Relative organizational level (management jobs)
- Type of people/work supervised (management jobs).

The new job-valuing frontier includes selecting the combination of elements that reflect the organization's skill and competency priorities and also provide an accurate relationship with market values. Also important is overcoming the weakness of individual compensation surveys, which often report compensation changes in market value that are due to changes in sample size and participants rather than real changes in the market. The use of multiple compensation surveys overcomes many of the problems of participation changes that plague the accuracy of individual compensation surveys. This is particularly important when employees can easily go on the Internet and get compensation survey data about their job.

Market Data

We have already introduced the problems with market data. The ideal solution is to have the organization that provides a job-valuing system based on the market also provide the data. The next generation of market-based job valuing should be managed on the Web, and this means access to quality databases as the foundation for the market. Without databases to support it, a job-valuing system based on market information is left open to outdated information. One of the advantages the Hay plan offered was a database of survey information from Hay plan users. This proved valuable to clients of the system. It provided information for them about how the clients valued jobs and how the factors translated into the market (although it averaged high and low markets for different jobs with the same job-evaluation points).

Some organizations believe that because of their importance to achieving key goals, certain jobs with no more market value than others are worth additional compensation dollars either in terms of base pay or incentive opportunity. "Strategic valuing" provides a way for organizations to assign value to people in key roles or with the organization's core competencies, based on the ways that they add more value. The tactic is to pay a premium over market for the most critical skills— assuming that organizations want to make sure they can get the best talent with the most essential skills and competencies by paying them above-market pay and perhaps offering above-market incentive opportunities.

Internet-based companies with salary products will likely have an advantage in the future of market valuing jobs, skills and competencies.

The Technology Factor

Technology has already begun to dominate HR where multiple information sources need to be managed, integrated and applied on a daily basis. This is true of job valuing where the external market is a primary platform for determining job worth. The following features will make up the coming generation of job valuing:

- **Web-Based:** The market-based system will be even more accessible on the Internet. The Web already provides secure access for HR professionals in some organizations, but the ease and use of the system will continue to progress. And administration of the job-valuing system through the Internet will become the standard.

- **Compensable Elements Aligned with Market Value:** The compensable elements to be used to value jobs will be selected based on their ability to align the values of jobs and skills with marketplace values. Scoring the jobs will result in placing jobs that cannot be accurately slotted by benchmarking into a pay category that reflects their value in the marketplace.

- **E-Survey Sources:** The data to be combined with the compensable elements must be available through the Internet. The user organizations must be able to combine the algorithm of the compensable elements with the market data to predict the value of all jobs included in the system. The survey data will permit a job-by-job ability to determine the market value of jobs on an as-needed basis.

- **Outsourceable to the Web:** The organization managing the job-valuing system will be able to outsource the entire system so it can be managed with little or no internal organizational resources.

- **Agile and Adaptable:** As things change in the market and inside the organization, market-based compensation can adapt accordingly. It also will provide the capability to strategically value jobs that are more important than the market predicts.

Paying for Skill and Competency on the Web

Organizations with an Internet presence, the data to correlate skill and competency with pay and the capability of managing pay on the Web could deliver a competency/skill-valuing pay solution. Although paying for skills may not totally replace job-based pay, it is likely that organizations are feeling limited by paying solely for jobs. Perhaps a gradual migration to paying for skills could occur over time. But skill/competency pay applications need to be simplified, which means a Web-based application.

The ideal solution would combine competencies and market information in a Web-based format that predicts the market value for an individual's combination of skills and competencies. This facilitates the development of skill libraries from which an individual's key skills and competencies can be identified. The list of skills/competencies needs to be flexible as these may change significantly over time.

Market pricing will eventually be linked with the skills library. Specific technical expertise is being market priced. In the IT function, a few survey companies provide market values for specific IT technical competencies. This will expand into other functional areas as the need arises—particularly as employers face a shortage of workers with the mass retirement of baby boomers.

Web-based technologies will facilitate this in several ways. As individuals provide data about their skills and competencies, this data can be used to determine the value of combinations of skills and competencies and eventually the value of the specific skills and competencies.

This solution will go beyond pay to all aspects of HR management. The readily quantifiable library of skills will allow for the assembly of the proper skill mix that reflects the work that needs to be done in the organization. This will link to performance management, succession planning, training and development, and selection. People will be "profileable" in terms of the skills and competencies they possess so they can choose, or be selected for, roles in the organization that best utilize their capabilities.

The People-Based Solution

Job valuing is changing from the current market-ranking solutions to a system where compensable elements become the powerful predictors of market value. The providers of these solutions will be organizations that presently have tools available on the Web and those that use the market to provide job pricing on an as-needed basis.

Most of the basic elements of these solutions are available but not integrated. The next generation is already on its way to realization. Job valuing will not be simple market ranking, but likely will be a solution that is defensible from a fairness standpoint and enables the total outsourcing of the system to avoid taxing internal resources. It also will eventually include a focus on skills and competencies. This innovation will be as important to the field of total compensation management as was the point-factor plan during the 1940s.

First published in *WorldatWork Journal*, Third Quarter 2005, 14 (3), 42-49.

CHAPTER 9:
Competencies and Rewards

After showing considerable promise in its introduction to pay and rewards, paying for competencies needs new energy and sponsorship to reach its potential. Paying for competencies means pay is influenced strongly by the competencies—the skills, knowledge and behaviors required to both perform a role and add value to a company—that a job needs, an employee offers and an employer rewards. Support for competency pay comes from advocates favoring the use of competencies the company needs to deliver results close to the core of the enterprise's business.

Companies differ in the capabilities they most urgently require to gain competitive business advantage. Some need competency/capability in the leading-edge technical area, some in lean manufacturing, whereas others need product marketing and start-up sales. Some definitions of competency focus on what is necessary for effective customer care or product and service quality, for example, but some other competencies are less readily described in specific terms. Companies often include competency and capability in their training and development efforts, focusing on internally creating the capability the company needs.

Recruitment and succession planning often rightfully emphasize competency and capability. Companies attempt to hire those who already have the competency profiles they need to help the company perform. All of this is often set in motion with the development of a company's "competency model" that commonly lists and defines the core competencies the company wants to drive its business and define itself as an employer.

Selecting Core Competencies

What competencies should be selected to gain competitive advantage? How should companies identify competencies? Does a company need a customized and proprietary competency model? A study of competency usage we conducted in 1996 showed that companies tend to emphasize some combination of the same competencies: customer focus, communication, team orientation, technical expertise, results orientation, leadership, adaptability and innovation. This suggests that advantage comes not so much from differences in competencies but from differences in the success of execution over time. So the secret is more than just choosing the right competencies—it is getting them into an action-oriented HR program that really works.

If companies want to use competencies to help brand their total rewards, they should streamline this process and make it business friendly and understandable.

Design

Because companies that adopt competencies sometimes build complex and sophisticated competency HR models, they often believe this investment of time, effort and expense should be used in the design of competency pay. But in nearly every instance, pay is the last element to be added to an already implemented competency HR solution.

Typically, the reasoning behind this is to get the complex competency applications for training, development, career development, succession planning, recruitment and performance management in place first and then the pay solution can be added, more positively. The problem is that by the time the company gets to the pay application, the competency program can be cumbersome, and many companies have not communicated to employees that pay will eventually be associated with the competency program.

The company may do an excellent job of accommodating the "softer" competency applications but fails to design the application to be pay user friendly. Because the competency design did not initially have the needs of a pay system in mind, it often turns out to be convoluted. And not keeping pay in mind from the start is a root cause of other problematic symptoms that can exist with competency pay. If competency-based pay is considered from the beginning—indeed if pay takes a lead role in the competency application—many of these challenges can be addressed early and effectively.

Clarity

Clear competency definitions put the entire competency program—ultimately including pay—on a stronger footing than vague and ambiguous ones. Poorly defined competencies and plans for acquiring and applying them are problems for programs such as career planning and development but are tragic for competency pay. Pay is a "hot" change vehicle—it gets the attention of everyone quickly and strongly. Pay makes either a positive or negative impression from the start. So any ambiguity creates the opportunity for negative "noise" about what makes or does not make sense to employees regarding how their pay is determined.

Employees may accept, for a time, a career development and training program that is not completely clear to them because the full impact seems so distant. But they are not as willing to accept an unclear and ill-defined foundation for their pay because the repercussions are immediate and evident.

It is important to consider some specifics. What is customer focus as a competency? How do you measure if people understand what it means in terms of behaviors and, if they do, if it is adding value to your organization? How about leadership? If you read 10 leadership books, you will likely get 10 different leadership definitions. And that applies to other competencies that companies try to define and use. Few people are willing to have their pay influenced based on an equivocal evaluation of their leadership skills, customer focus, or whatever competency is being "measured." Company leaders must understand and carefully define competencies important to the organization.

Connected to the Labor Market

Competency pay should be connected with the realities of the external marketplace. Very few pay surveys compare jobs based on the competencies or capabilities required to perform them. Even skills that are more concrete—specific technical, clerical, financial, scientific and other skills needed for jobs like technicians, administrative assistants, financial analysts, scientists, nurses and others—are not surveyed, but rather the job is surveyed for competitive practice. Surveys focus on the semantics of describing jobs, and this connotes paying job incumbents merely for being assigned to jobs, not for any actual skill and capability to perform them. Exceptions to this are a few IT surveys that focus on technical competencies rather than jobs.

What happens in most instances is the competency pay result is compared to the external market on the back end of the study process. This amounts to ranking the job relative to the marketplace and essentially ignoring the differences in competency levels among the individual incumbents. The absence of a link between the competency pay solution and the market worth of jobs, or specifically the market worth of competencies, is a major problem. The difficulty with this is the potential for accelerated pay inflation. If the problems of complexity, overdesign, vagueness and ambiguity exist, it is difficult to determine if employees have actually acquired and applied a competency. So companies will give employees the benefit of the doubt, and this may make competency pay expensive.

Championed and Communicated

Few executives have ever been paid under competency-based pay solutions. People sponsor what they like and are accustomed to. It is very difficult to convince others that something is worth doing if you are not doing it yourself. Most executives who would be called on to sponsor and communicate a pay solution have been paid based on the job they hold rather than the competencies they possess. Would you suggest to employees that they should highly value stock options when you do not have options yourself? The credibility of what you are suggesting is at stake.

Executives need help concerning how best to give continuing sponsorship for competencies, including education about how competency pay works and about how to educate others. In too many instances, the lead supporters deliver the same message repeatedly. Keeping sponsorship fresh and interesting is the name of the game. You must keep everyone interested and focused—and that means the champions as well as the employees to whom the primary communications message is directed. For example, updating a "book of lore" of situations in which employees demonstrate competencies at a role-model level serves as a recognition and educational tool.

Competency Pay Going Forward
More Value

The power and positive future of paying for competencies rests with our ability to address the issues we have summarized. The overall concept should be more business practical and user friendly. The most pressing challenge for competency pay is linkage with the external marketplace. The few surveys that try to exchange data based on skill and competency are difficult to work with, and providing data to the surveys is complex and burdensome. Managing competency pay systems is a task for everyone involved. So although these systems sound great and are certainly focused on the "right stuff" from the standpoint of what companies should pay for, they must be made easier to use.

So where is the benefit for a company to maintain a system that pays for competencies and not just for jobs? We can show that companies that provide incentives for achieving certain goals that are within the influence of employees are more likely to see these goals met than are companies that do not pay for goal achievement, but the same cannot be said for paying for competencies. And the real challenge is the possibility that companies will continue to design and implement competency-based HR solutions for other uses (recruitment, performance management, training and development, succession and career development and the like) and not use the same systems to drive their pay solution. This means the pay solution will be based on something other than the aim of the other people-management systems.

Positive Evidence

Companies often need concrete evidence of viability to deploy HR programs that affect pay. The litmus test of all HR applications may be to determine if the company is willing to use the same foundation for pay as it does for anything else related to people. And if the company decides that whatever systems it would like to use for other applications do not fit for pay, then whatever pay solution it is using will erode everything else it does because pay and other communication messages are not aligned. For example, if pay is based on "jobs" with an annual "merit" system, this may have nothing to do with the competencies the company is encouraging people to obtain and apply to perform their work. It is more likely that the people will do whatever they believe will most influence their pay rather than emphasize a HR learning experience that is difficult and seemingly unrelated to pay.

Keeping Best People

An agenda for companies is how to deal with superkeepers. These high-performing people possess not only the competencies the company needs to be an effective business competitor but also the proven ability to translate these capabilities into measurable business outcomes. Although seldom comprising more than 20 percent of the workforce, they should have priority claim on compensation and reward dollars in competitive business times. And competency pay is potentially an essential tool in helping companies to identify and reward these critical people consistent with their value to the business. This makes pragmatic competency pay an even more powerful business tool and provides a new priority for rewards planners to make competency pay work much more effectively.

Strategic Initiative

Indeed, we believe that a powerful business case for competency pay that focuses on the more important competencies from our 1996 article can be made on the basis of superkeepers alone. A priority for rewards planners is to gain access to their company's "strategic business suite" where key directions and how to bring them to fruition are fashioned. And what better way to add value to a company than to suggest a tool that will help company leadership identify and define the few most important competencies the organization needs, determine who has these competencies along with the ability to translate them into results, and establish a way to reward these superkeepers objectively and meaningfully through a total rewards solution that places a premium value on your company's most essential talent.

So the future opportunity will be to take a great concept—paying for competencies—and make it practical and usable. If companies consider competencies as a tool to determine pay at the start of the evaluation process, we can see more competency-based HR solutions. Competencies are valuable and need added business substance to serve as the strong foundation for an entire HR strategy—which must include linking pay and rewards to business goals.

Revised October 2006; first published in *Compensation & Benefits Review*, September/October 2003, 35 (5), 40-44. Reprinted by permission of SAGE Publications Inc.

CHAPTER 10:
Assessing the Value of Skill-Based Pay

The total rewards model includes individual growth as a rewards component. Skill growth provides a dimension of how to best align employees' efforts with goal performance. Paying for skill and competency is essential to designing base pay that rewards individual ongoing value and, to create a win-win situation for organizations and employees, rewards solutions should be built around the skills and competencies that businesses need and that employees obtain and apply to achieve business results.

The logic of skill-based pay overpowers that of job-based pay from a conceptual perspective but has struggled, causing some companies to hesitate pursuing it for their organizations. Complexity is a primary issue because skill-based pay requires clarity in the following:

- How to derive skill definitions
- How skills are acquired, demonstrated and assessed
- How and when skills should be paid
- How new skills are learned while sustaining/improving business performance
- When new skills replace obsolete skills.

Skill-based pay is also hard to relate to competitive practice because nearly all of the most popular surveys report on what jobs are worth in the market, not the worth of skills and capabilities. Because market pay has grown in popularity, it is difficult to move forward confidently with a pay solution that has had as many publicized failures as successes.

Some highly successful skill-based pay installations exist in manufacturing, but manufacturing is in a slump, thereby putting pressure on even the most workable and value-added skill-based pay solutions. Some other nonexempt populations have skill-based pay—for example, customer service representatives in contact or call centers where being able to answer all the customer's questions in one phone call, instead of transferring them, is important to customer satisfaction.

Organizations, however, may be hesitant to experiment when pay solutions based on market value are working well. With concerns about labor costs, businesses are not inclined to move to a pay foundation perceived as too complex and adding cost although it may increase employee satisfaction and reduce turnover. Because skill-based pay has struggled, it likely will be necessary to over-prove its value.

Kick Start Skill-Based Pay

Organizations need to insist that the program be simple to explain and must match the communication concept of the "elevator speech." (If a trainer gets on an elevator on the ground floor of a 20-story building with someone else, that other individual should have a solid general understanding of how the program applies to him or her by the time they reach the top floor.)

A skill-based pay program should include:

- Skills and competencies—directly important to job performance—that can be defined in measurable and objective terms
- Skills that employees apply on the job to achieve desirable job performance objectives. Employers should pay for performance, not training.
- New and different skills that replace obsolete skills or skills that no longer are important to job performance. Skills should be periodically reviewed to stay up-to-date and relevant to business needs.
- On-the-job skill training, not "in the classroom." Those who possess the skills should teach them. Also, include on-the-job assessment, which can be supplemented by paper-and-pencil exams administered on the job, as well.

These solutions should be implemented with the understanding that it may take several years for skill-based pay to bear fruit for the company and its employees. It is just a different way for companies and employees to think about pay.

Initially, skill-based pay seems to increase the cost of the employees included in the program. Transition charges often are considerable, and the overall labor cost relationship also can be a significant challenge. Kick starting skill-based pay likely means building a new body of knowledge on what does—and does not—work. It also requires defining the reasons companies should consider it (e.g., what to expect in return for the time and resources required for installation). Also, more realistic timelines need to be developed for skill-based pay implementation from project startup to the realization of benefits.

Cranking up the Engine

Businesses can consider skill-based pay as part of any total rewards solution. There are technical issues and challenges of workforce involvement, acceptance and commitment. An organization can perform pre-approval processes on skill-based pay with the following steps:

- **Justify the application.** Determine the expected advantages derived from a skill-based pay program early. The most probable expectations are to encourage a more flexible workforce that seeks learning and uses needed skills and capabilities to perform effectively, along with a solution that pays more as people learn more and apply newfound skills to the job to achieve business results. Consider: Are these reasons enough to make implementing a skill-based pay program worth the effort?

- **Determine readiness.** Determine if the company is ready, or can prepare, for skill-based pay. Consider different scenarios about how pay and rewards issues will be managed in an environment where people are paid for the skills they have, can obtain and will apply to produce results, rather than for the jobs they already have or may not accurately fit.

- **Prepare for change.** How has the organization addressed major change regarding HR policy and programs in the past? Moreover, has it been tasked to address changes relative to people issues?

- **Define tolerances.** Decide if the organization is willing to do what it takes to design, implement, communicate and manage a skill-based pay solution on a continual basis. What is the company's tolerance if this workforce change creates noise? Will leadership, aided by change supporters, have the patience to wait for its acceptance? Is any pain during the change process worth the effort?

- **Establish the plan and timelines.** Once the decision to proceed has been made (if it has been made), foster commitment to a plan for implementing skill-based pay, including specific timelines. Communicate the plan to those involved, describing the reasons for the decision and how the process will unfold. Do not plan on wishful thinking, but on your best estimate of the magnitude and challenge.

- **Follow the plan.** Act on what has been developed and work to make it successful. If adjustments need to be made along the way for unexpected occurrences, make them. Tell employees what is happening and why, and get the process moving steadily and as close to on time and on target as possible.

Preparation is essential when it has been determined that skill-based pay makes sense for an organization. Success does not need to be defined in terms of implementing a skill-based pay solution. It may result in *not* implementing skill-based pay, and it may result in moving to a solution that differs from the current plan, but does not include a total skill-based pay answer.

Where Skill-Based Pay Can Add Most Value

Here are some possible skill-based pay applications where skill-based pay is a viable business solution for pay management:

- A company whose leadership has a realistic understanding of skill-based pay's challenges and opportunities, particularly from the perspective of how much time and energy it will take to make skill-based pay operational.
- An environment in which a skill progression exists and skills higher in this progression are more valuable to the business and to the employee than other skills.
- Situations where skills are concrete and can be defined so everyone knows when someone has the skill and when they do not. Where little controversy exists about who has and applies the skill to achieve business results.
- Circumstances where the opportunities for growth and rotation are not encumbered by arbitrary work rules and seniority systems that are "anti-skill."
- Organizations where employee involvement, strong communications and mutual trust exist.
- Where experimental HR systems can be explored.
- Where, if the solution does not work, the HR situation is such that more experimentation is possible in the future.

Businesses somehow do not seem to be seeing a fit between skill-based pay and the problems they are facing concerning pay at this time. Perhaps skill-based pay is a "good time" answer that cannot stand the test of economic challenge. It is more likely that a solution for base pay that survives the need to create a high-performance business will focus on the actual people who have the most important skills and capabilities. The jury is still out on whether this will be some type of skill-based pay.

If skill-based pay can emphasize a value-added business formula by responding to both the skills the company needs for success and the market value of these skills, then some form of skill-based pay probably will have lasting value to the enterprise. It must link to results—either paired with incentives or require a level of performance and results to pay for a particular skill. Skill-based pay also needs to be more streamlined and easier to understand and communicate. And companies must have very clear and realistic expectations as to what it can deliver.

Revised October 2006; first published in *WorldatWork Journal*, Third Quarter 2002, 11 (3), 72-77.

CHAPTER 11:

Business Value, Paying for Skill and the Internet

The context of pay and rewards innovation has evolved dramatically in response to an expanding and changing global community and economy. Going forward, pay and rewards designs must be defined in terms of adding value to the business. The question, of course, is whether or not they will. Often organizations recognize a need for new rewards directions but are sometimes slower to execute new alignments than to acknowledge the need to change. Prior generations of invention brought us such great tools as variable pay, performance shares, cascading goals for performance management and multisource performance feedback. However, the strong connection between rewards design and business goals has been elusive. Whatever rewards designers think of it, the U.S. Sarbanes-Oxley Act of 2002 placed a more urgent priority on linking rewards and goal performance. So the "now" generation of pay and rewards should reflect a much tighter relationship between business outcomes and rewards.

Another essential innovation on the fast track is more efficient pay and rewards management. Because of organizational streamlining and staff reductions, businesses lack the legions of support people they once had to administer complex pay and rewards systems. Professionals once responsible for writing job descriptions and pricing jobs are now often assigned to such important accountabilities as coaching managers on how best to manage employee performance and how to more strongly differentiate pay adjustments based on the value added to the organization, skills and performance. This leaves organizations with a goal of implementing more effective and streamlined rewards solutions that can be more readily managed. Streamlining the administration of pay and rewards is an essential priority, and the solution rests with the Internet.

Innovation should, in our view, focus both on a key business issue and on making pay and rewards solutions more efficient. We suggest a combination:

- **Paying for Skills:** The rebirth and revitalization of pay and rewards solutions that permit organizations to pay for jobs where that makes sense but also to pay for skills when that best fits their needs. Enabling paying for skills is a key priority for the next few years. This involves paying for skills for not only manufacturing and other nonexempt jobs but also exempt jobs where skills and competencies are critical for outcomes.
- **Web Management of Pay and Rewards:** "Out-Webbing" pay and rewards administration to the Internet. Developing Web-based support systems for pay solutions like skill pay that more efficiently manage pay and rewards.

The Skills Four-Legged Stool

Although paying for skills and competencies may not totally replace job-based pay, it is likely that enough organizations are feeling limited by paying just for jobs that a gradual migration to paying for skills and competencies could occur over time. But these pay applications need to be much simplified, and easier to explain and understand. We think this means an Internet application.

The urgent need to make the business use of skills more practical is not just a pay issue. Training, development, succession planning, performance management, recruitment, selection, placement and nearly every HR issue organizations face need to evaluate skills. Skills and the ability to translate them into performance are the cornerstones of contemporary HR management. As seen in Exhibit 11-1, skills form the foundation of a "four-legged stool" for organizations.

EXHIBIT 11-1 **The Skills Four-Legged Stool**

Development and Training	Performance Management and Assessment
Succession Planning, Staffing, Recruitment	Pay and Rewards

Pay and Rewards

The stakes for providing a solution for the management of skills are huge. This is especially true in the United States where the focus is on improving organizational performance and providing attractive work. Everything is linked to the skills that organizations need and people provide. Making a skill-based talent management solution practical is more than just important.

What is needed is a skill solution that goes beyond pay to all aspects of HR management. This requires the development of a readily assessable library of skills that can be used by organizations and people to assemble the skill mix that reflects the work to be done in the organization. As the need for skills changes and new skills emerge, the library must adapt. Skills must be "priceable" in the external market so people and organizations have an idea of what their skills are worth. Organizations must be able to pay most for skills that are both most valuable in the marketplace and worth the most to the business. Businesses must be able to utilize job-based systems in one part of the organization and skill-based systems in another, and be able to relate people in one system to those in another. And organizations need to move people from system to system without creating extreme discord and disruption.

All the skill-based HR systems must be linkable. That means performance management and succession planning are tied to skill learning and development. People must be "profileable" in terms of the skills they possess. People with specific skills should be able to seek work that needs those skills. And organizations that need specific skill sets must be able to find the people who have these skills. How well skills are applied to do work must be discernible. There is more, but we think you get the picture. The move to skills requires the application of current, timesaving and readily accessible technology.

Internet and Paying for Skills

A number of useful pay and rewards tools are available on the Internet. The most practical are those that permit an organization or individual to determine the "going market rate" for specific jobs. The Web also has good general and specific survey information plus leads on how to get data on what dollar amounts jobs are paid. But so far the Web doesn't feature any really powerful tools and programs to facilitate how, not what, people are paid. For example, organizations cannot find a Web-based variable pay program or a job evaluation program that can be purchased and adapted to business needs. Should the Internet have products such as this? And what might be the most pressing Web application needed for pay management?

Available Internet tools to date focus only on jobs and not skills. Several Internet companies have sliced and diced information on jobs, careers and pay. Each developed excellent Internet tools that do everything to build the four-legged stool except being able to objectively address the skills foundation. And certainly none are able to determine the individual market value of the skills.

What will the tools for Internet skill pay look like? All present solutions have the potential to meet the needs of paying for skills. The needs of an Internet skill pay solution include the following:

- **Skills Library:** An Internet-based way to access well-defined skill combinations in order to determine what skills are needed to perform in a specific organizational role and to use the definitions in the skills library to define the basic elements of work. The definitions should be concrete and based on real skill differences, not merely semantic differentials. The skill definitions should be standardized to provide a future for a large survey of the market value of specific skills.

- **Skill Profiling Capability:** Based on the skills library, a way to develop accurate skill profiles that combine multiple skills and skill sets to match how work is actually performed in an organization. This provides profiles that combine skills commonly appearing together in work situations—and permits the organization to add or delete skills flexibly from a role being assigned to an individual to reflect actual skills needed to perform the required work.

- **Methodologies for Market Pricing Skills:** Solutions for approximating the market value of skills from the measured market value of defined jobs include: 1) estimating the value of skills from the value of jobs that normally require these skills; 2) ultimately being able to directly survey the market value of skills defined in the library and in skill profiles; 3) permitting organizations to anchor skill pay solutions in the market; and 4) preventing possible inflation of skill pay costs that may result from the absence of market information that guides the payment of certain skill combinations.

- **Skill Pay Programming:** A system for paying people for the skills they have and use to perform the work they are assigned. This system links the skills library, the skill profile of the individual, and surveys or approximating the market value of skills and skill profiles to how much the individual is paid. The solution will have mechanics of how people's pay is adjusted, how the acquisition of skills is paid for, how the application of skills is rewarded, what happens when skills become obsolete and people need to acquire new skills, and the like. It is the "how paying for skills works" part of the process.

- **Skill Performance Management:** A methodology for evaluating skill competence and skill performance that results in the individual's work performance. The methodology encompasses: 1) standards of skill performance that can be evaluated by multiple means such as observation, work samples, testing, and in-work performance reviews; 2) linkages between the performance management outcome and other skill-based HR tools; and 3) tools that translate the acquisition and application of skills into performance. Further, the methodology provides guidelines that suggest what happens when a skill is learned, defines the importance of a skill and how fast the skill is learned, and helps the performance process by making qualitative and quantitative judgments about how well the skill is learned and applied.

- **Skill Training and Development:** Teaching tools for skill development including: 1) online education for managers to use to train people and for individual self-learning to develop the needed skills; 2) teaching solutions that adapt to changes in skill needs; and 3) linkages to performance management and paying for skills to permit testing and evaluation as well as pay for accomplishment. This relates training and development to the process of evaluating whether or not the individual is performing at a satisfactory level, and also provides tools for skill improvement if skill is deficient.

- **Succession and Advancement:** Skill progression tools that help create a way to move to work that requires more complex and challenging skills the organization's business specifically needs. This would include 1) developing career paths that are associated with skills with information on how important and difficult to acquire and apply the skills are; 2) making changes to how people grow and add value that are focused on demonstrating needed skills rather than jobs and job titles; and 3) communicating a route for people to follow to higher pay and more of the critical skills.

- **Recruitment, Selection, and Placement:** Tools to help attract the people with the needed skills to the organization and subsequently select and provide them work that utilizes those skills effectively. These tools would: 1) provide methodologies that set a priority of keeping people with critical skills in the event of talent cutbacks; 2) facilitate the evaluation of skills and hiring people with specific skills; and 3) permit focusing on hiring people that satisfy skill needs, not just people who have held jobs with similar-sounding titles in other organizations.

This seems a tall order for an HR program with a foundation of skills—but not really a major challenge for an Internet application. It combines the features organizations have developed and implemented by means of manual skill-based HR solutions but are not linked or integrated. Most of these program elements exist in either HRIS systems or on PC-based systems. The key issue is one of HR applications on the Internet.

The Internet has not proven to be a highly viable way to get products in the hands of users when the product is administered and monitored on the Internet, however. The challenge of managing confidential pay and rewards data on the Web can probably be addressed by some sort of intranet tool that translates Internet information into a tool applied within the organization.

Problems the Web Solves on Paying for Skills

"The philosophy of paying for skills is beautiful, but implementation and management are a nightmare," says one of the most respected rewards advisers. First, most critics believe that the HRIS systems on the market are not designed to manage a pay system based on the skills individuals possess. Secondly they believe that skill pay is one of the most over-engineered of all possible HR systems. Because paying for skills rather than jobs is so different from what people are accustomed to, organizations developing such solutions are more likely than not to develop them with considerable employee and management involvement. And because most organizations that are implementing such programs do not have experience with such solutions, the design becomes very involved.

The Web can provide relatively standardized tools that can be adapted to meet the needs of a specific organization. Tools such as a skills library, distance learning for skill training and development, and methodologies for market pricing skills are made for Internet applications. These are the things that organizations try to unnecessarily build from scratch, that consume time and energy and create frustration and confusion. The Internet allows the organization developing skill pay to spend its time on customizing the solutions to meet its needs. This will make paying for skills practical and permit out-Webbing of the functions that are best moved outside the organization.

Conclusion

This is a good time to challenge providers of Internet HR tools to develop something they are well qualified to deliver. Organizations are in dire need of a pay solution that matches the interest businesses have in making skills the foundation of HR planning. And at the core of it is paying for skills. Skill pay made great business sense except for the problems that the Internet is ideally suited to solving.

We already have providers of survey data on the Web. What we need is someone to step forward to develop and implement something that will provide organizations with the next innovation in compensation. And that could be a practical and streamlined way to implement paying for skills. Not that this will completely replace paying for jobs. However, for some organizations, it is likely a way to encourage people to acquire and apply the skills that most help the organization be successful. And, in the final analysis, that is what a pay program should do to be deemed a success. The next generation of pay and rewards innovation will be closer to the business of organizations than prior innovations. And it is likely that a combination of the Internet and paying for the skills that add value to the business may just be how the future will be defined.

First published in *IHRIM Journal*, September/October 2004, VIII (5), 47-50.

PART IV
Making Positive Change

CHAPTER 12

Sales Rewards Solutions

Sales and profitability are always under pressure, so substantial opportunity exists for the salesforce to add value. To drive high performance, companies should periodically review and possibly rejuvenate selling strategies and tactics to regain or enhance selling traction. Many give considerable attention to how best to implement sales incentive plans to march new drives for selling momentum. But companies should also realign their selling rewards solutions to their business plans to enhance sales or restore sales performance to satisfactory levels. Sales compensation may need some short-term attention and perhaps a tune-up. (See Exhibit 12-1.)

Paying Selling Professionals

One of the ongoing problems in the world of total rewards is how to compensate an active and important field salesforce. Whether the selling professionals are selling individually or in teams, selling large- or small-ticket items or selling to many customers or just a few important ones, paying them raises difficult issues. This is especially so for HR professionals who have made inroads into providing support to sales compensation design or those who want to provide help as part of their total rewards agenda for a company. Once the turf of only the front-line selling organizations, designing sales compensation is a growing role for HR practitioners and rewards designers, which is bringing valuable returns for the selling enterprise.

The range of sales compensation designs is wide. Some sales professionals are paid only base salaries and others only commissions on sales. And any combination of base pay and incentives or commissions is possible. From a strategic perspective, the key is matching a sales compensation design to how a company patterns its selling strategy as part of the overall business plan. A company needs to build a powerful business case for the role sales professionals play in the success of the business and for the methodology as well as the amount they are paid for doing what they do.

EXHIBIT 12-1 **Time for a High-Performance Sales Pay Tune-Up?**

Companies are challenged to improve performance. Here are some energizing and positive ideas you can use without a major change to your company's sales compensation solution:

- **Ensure the opportunity for competitive total cash compensation based on results.** In most companies, strong-performing sales professionals are superkeepers. Make sure the strong-performing sales professionals have at least competitive total cash compensation to keep them in your company. Competitive compensation should correspond to stretch but achievable goal performance with strongly competitively compensation for those with outstanding performance.

- **Ensure a proper base-incentive mix based on selling conditions.** Is the relationship between base pay and incentives right? Do the sales role, selling situation and prominence of the salesforce in the marketing mix suggest more or less incentive or base pay? If you have reasonable goals and want to "juice" the selling professionals, maybe a larger portion of incentive in the mix is called for. If it is new capabilities and behaviors, maybe more base pay relative to the mix is needed.

- **Update incentive measures and goals consistent with the business plan.** Are the measures for sales incentives the right ones? Does your company need to worry about more than just sales volume goals? Maybe new customers, greater penetration, the retention of existing customers or new markets? Take some time to redefine what your company needs and what your sales professionals should deliver. It is worth the effort.

- **Set realistic performance goals, given business conditions.** Every company hopes to outperform last year. But this may not make sense during tough performance years. So, look at the realities of the sales goals. In some instances, just matching last year's performance will do the trick. In years of a strong economy, market growth conditions, or strong new company products and services relative to competitors, goals are set higher. The name of the game is stretch but achievable sales goal setting.

- **Update target customers.** Who are your customers and are they the right ones in terms of the profitability and long-term growth of your company? Some companies are looking to broader customer bases because they are moving away from just competing with their toughest competition for the same customers.

- **Reinforce critical selling behaviors and capabilities.** Are your sales professionals doing what you want them to do? Do they need to learn and apply new behaviors and capabilities to your business process as the selling situation changes? Should you begin to pay for new capabilities and directions? It is essential to define the selling job and compare it with the outcomes and behaviors you are getting from your talent resources.

Although these issues are at the core of selling performance, our objective here is more tactical than strategic. We want to provide some ideas for a quicker fix, even though the diagnosis may end up suggesting the need for major strategic change. Note the emphasis on "quicker" rather "quick," because even fixes such as we are suggesting take time and patience.

Tuning Up Sales Compensation

So your job as a HR adviser is to update the sales compensation program in short order. Here are some ideas you should consider for your sales compensation tuneup:

- Ensure the opportunity for competitive total cash compensation based on results
- Ensure a proper base-incentive mix based on selling conditions
- Update incentive measures and goals consistent with the business plan
- Set realistic performance goals, given business conditions
- Update target customers
- Reinforce critical selling behaviors and capabilities.

Although there may be other tune-up opportunities, addressing these six will give you the chance to restart and recommunicate new priorities and urgencies to your frontline selling force.

Ensure Competitive Total Cash

Superkeepers are people your company must keep and get more of in good times and bad times because they are strong performers and possess core competencies that are critical to the business and give the company a differential advantage. In most businesses, members of the field salesforce are candidates for superkeeper status. Pay increase budgets may likely stay at 3.5 percent to 4 percent for the next few years. Our tip is to make sure that the combination of whatever base pay sales professionals receive and their incentive opportunities as a result of achieving realistic goals given the business conditions provides the opportunity for competitive total cash compensation. If not, we suggest that the salesforce who often possess key core competencies of the company may need to receive a larger share of whatever pay dollars the company has to distribute. This may mean more base pay dollars, more upside incentive opportunity or a combination of the two. Or this may mean higher upside incentive opportunity that is earned by the top performers.

Your company may need to upgrade the selling workforce. Top-selling talent is in demand. But some companies let excellent people go for reasons other than performance, and this talent may have directly applicable experience your company can put to work in short order. But a word of warning—make sure you are not picking up another company's "talent leavings." Check carefully. Many businesses weed out poor performers, and you might do this as well. You don't want to replace your people with the "weeds" pulled by other companies. Pay is a major cost, and you must direct it to superkeepers—who often include sales talent.

Ensure a Proper Base-Incentive Mix

A part of competitive pay is how the sales compensation elements are assembled— how much of the total pay opportunity varies on the basis of selling performance, how much is in the form of base pay and what causes base pay to change? For example, some sales roles have changed to more consultative selling with greater relationship management responsibility—coordinating a selling team to solve customers' problems. For these jobs, the mix may need to change to more base pay and less incentive. Or the objective may be to emphasize new behaviors and capabilities that can best be acknowledged through additional base pay for some period of time. Alternatively, a company's objective may be to reach a broader market base through telephone sales representatives who can handle smaller customers and less complex repeat-business transactions. The mix for these sales professionals may need to change to less base pay and more incentive.

Obviously, more base pay provides an increasingly predictable compensation result. So, if measures and goals for incentives are unstable, changing or unpredictable, changing the mix to more base pay and less incentive may be appropriate. A startup company that has grown to a point at which sales volumes are more predictable may change the mix to more base pay and less incentive. Also, if the company's reputation and advertising have become more prominent elements in the marketing mix relative to the salesforce than before, then the mix can change to more base pay and less incentive.

In contrast, new sales goals with limited histories or proven track records, such as introducing new products or entering new markets, suggest lowering the point at which incentives begin to be earned and transitioning to a mix with less base pay and more incentive. It is important for rewards planners to make sure that the total cash compensation mix fits with the evolving selling situation and reflects changes in sales roles, marketing mix, products and markets.

Update Incentive Measures

You get what you pay for—that is especially true in the realm of sales compensation. And it is possible that you may tactically want something different from what you hoped for when the current plan was put in place. Assume that one incentive measure is sales volume performance compared with the goal. Perhaps the new priority is improvement over last year or even keeping up with the sales volume from last year, depending on the business situation in your industry. Maybe a goal is to grow the business foundation in existing customers or to add new customers to those to whom your company already sells. Or to open new markets for existing or new products or to change the product mix or introduce new products. Looking to the company's business plan will provide some important clues as to how the sales professionals can help the company restore performance momentum.

Typically, the sales compensation goal is overall sales volume. Perhaps additional goals other than sales volume are needed to direct the salesforce to achieve the company's business plan. We see goals that focus on selling specific products and services, customer retention and margin/profit as part of sales incentives.

Do you have the right measures and goals? Are they individual or shared goals? Do the sales professionals directly affect the goals (close line-of-sight goals) or merely influence the goals in some way (longer line-of-sight goals)? Are the sales professionals to expend effort on one or two primary goals or on more goals? The more goals the sales professionals have to focus on, the more diffused the selling effort will be.

Most companies will list the three to five most important company goals from tactical and strategic perspectives. Next, they will determine which of these goals the salesforce can best influence. Then, this process can evaluate what the incentive plans currently pay for compared with these new goals. On the basis of this analysis, any changes in sales measures and goals can be considered.

Set Realistic Performance Goals

Many companies set selling goals based on the business plan. Sometimes these goals are set more on the basis of what companies need (or hope for) in terms of selling performance than what is possible, given the current competitive and business circumstances. Sales incentive plans should focus on realistic performance expectations compared to a combination of business plan, business conditions and prior year's performance.

Sales incentive plans must be affordable to the company, given the results achieved. Sales goals should not become a "slam dunk" such that little selling effort results in competitive awards. In this situation, sales targets should be set higher, as well as the performance levels above target. If the salesforce is comfortable hitting sales targets and does not push for sales above target, the slope of the incentive line may also be too flat above target and incentive opportunities may need to be increased above target to drive the added sales, particularly if these "last" added sales revenues measurably increase the company's bottom line.

On the other hand, in some years, companies may find that sales performance that just maintains the prior year's performance is excellent and should be rewarded, given the business, product and service situations in a competitive market. Otherwise, if incentives based on sales success constitute a large element of compensation, sales professionals may be dramatically underpaid when business realities are considered. The selling situation may be that your company cannot expect to improve annually on selling performance every year.

Even if sales targets are a challenge in a down year, there are likely incentive-worthy sales goals that result in business improvement. In a multiple-goal plan, for example, improvement may be made in the types and number of customers to whom a company sells in a specific territory. Often, we see situations in which unrealistic sales volume expectations are projected in the current year compared with the prior year. And when the sales professionals fail to achieve the established goals, exceptions are made, and they receive at least partial incentive payments anyway. This may erode trust in the incentive plan going forward. So, it is best to set realistic performance expectations rather than to set goals on the basis of wishful thinking relative to projected performance.

So, part of the tune-up process is to address the results/reward relationship between sales incentives and stretch but achievable sales goals compared to business plan, business conditions, and the prior year's performance. And it is important to make sure that there is sufficient upside incentive opportunity for those who have outstanding sales performance—the superkeepers. This keeps the salesforce "in the hunt" for outstanding performance.

Update Target Customers

Who are your company's customers? Have they changed? Do they need to change? Is your plan to sell more to existing customers or to find new customers? Challenging times often cause companies to explore these important questions of which customers are currently and potentially the most profitable. Typically, this has led to the conclusion that it is less costly and more profitable to sell to existing customers who fit a specific model that makes them attractive. However, these same customers may also be the targets of your competition.

Redefining the customer base can be a fruitful undertaking when the competition for profitable sales is high. Many companies evaluate customers in terms of the cost of sales and profitability. They emphasize selling to customers for whom the cost of doing so is lowest compared with the income and return on sales. This often changes during competitive times, when companies may find that redefining target customers, even for a short period, is worthwhile.

For example, a niche technology company with only a few customers lost a major order from one of them for a specific product. It would be several years before the selling opportunity to this specific customer could arise again. Leadership decided that it was less expensive in terms of selling cost to slightly redefine the product and approach to customers to be somewhat out of the niche into which the company had sold for many years. Although this was more costly than selling to existing customers, the additional expense was more than offset by the expanded selling opportunities and expanded market that the new target customers offered to the organization. Sales incentives reinforced this new direction into new markets by changing the weighting of incentive opportunities toward this new direction.

Reinforce Critical Selling Behaviors

What sort of selling behaviors do you want from your selling professionals? What is their role in making sales? Is it changing? If so, how and why? Are they responsible for making sales and turning them over to others in the company? Or do they have an obligation to follow up and manage the delivery of the products or services? Also, do customers expect periodic contact with the sales professionals, or is it the professionals' responsibility to make the sales and move on to seek and sell to other customers? Is the role of the sales professionals educational relative to the products or services or problem solving relative to specific customer issues, or are the products or services more commodities that are purchased principally on the basis of price? And importantly, is the need for new required behaviors and capabilities evolving slowly or rapidly?

Companies are evaluating what they get for any base pay they provide in addition to variable selling incentives. One observable trend is to associate base pay adjustments with performance management tools that focus closely on the behaviors and capabilities companies want to develop in their professional selling forces. For instance, a performance management system can focus on the learning and application of new skills and be tied to future pay adjustments that are contingent on acceptable performance in these dimensions.

Suggestions and Opportunities

Pay is a powerful communicator of performance directions and company values. And most professional salesforces are especially sensitive to what their companies pay them for. So, in times demanding an increased focus on company performance, evaluating the sales compensation plan is one thing to put on your list. The main reason, of course, is to get the message through to your frontline people about the company's key priorities and how they can help make these a reality.

It may be that a major change in how sales rewards are configured is in the offing. But a change here and there without a major redesign of the entire selling rewards solution can very often generate the types of results a company expects when it needs maximum leverage from what it pays selling professionals.

Revised October 2006; first published in *Compensation & Benefits Review*, September/October 2004, 36 (5), 21-26. Reprinted by permission of SAGE Publications Inc.

CHAPTER 13:
Executive Compensation: Doing the 'Heavy Lifting'

An HR leader is communicating to the general workforce about freezing benefits and terminating the company's qualified defined-benefit pension plan, due in part to recent changes to federal legislation. She states the business case for change as one of competition from lower labor-cost providers, and the reasons for change seem sound. An employee in the audience asks why the executive officers' retirement is so large and increasing considerably in comparison to his own retirement, which will be decreasing. He had just seen in the most recent proxy the top officers' dollar values in their supplemental executive retirement plan (SERP).

If you head HR at a public company and think this scenario does not pertain to you, think again. It is going to play out more frequently with the increased executive compensation disclosure requirements unanimously approved by the U.S. Securities and Exchange Commission in July 2006.

The future will demand increased alignment of the messages of compensation between the workforce and executives, and an emphasis on truly paying for performance. For executive compensation, this means a more holistic focus on total rewards or total compensation rather than specific individual elements. Also required are a reinforcement of the pay-for-performance linkage and a stronger role for HR leaders in influencing the CEO on executive compensation direction.

The SEC disclosure rules will reinforce the holistic approach. Performance shares, a long-term compensation tool, meanwhile, can enhance the pay-for-performance relationship. HR leaders wanting to contribute in a strategic way must address the "heavy lifting" of dealing with the compensation of company leaders.

Total Compensation Perspective

SEC's proxy disclosure rules about executive compensation enable investors, employees and other interested parties to review a named executive officer's total compensation, creating a transparency previously unavailable.

Pundits view its impact differently. On one hand, Jeffrey Pfeffer, professor of organizational behavior at Stanford University's School of Business, believes pay should be more private because, with disclosure, executives will want to match other executives' higher total compensation. We believe, on the other hand, that greater transparency is positive. Compensation should be reviewed not piecemeal by each element—but as a whole. This increases understanding not only of the total value, but also of how the elements are balanced—e.g., the proportion of performance-based versus nonperformance-based compensation and long-term compensation versus short-term compensation.

The SEC disclosure rules will also result in a stronger focus on performance-based compensation in the future. Among other changes, companies now include in the summary total compensation calculation the annual change in the actuarial present value of accumulated pension benefits from all executive and qualified retirement plans and the above-market or preferential earnings on nonqualified deferred compensation of each of the five named executive officers. Another chart shows the actuarial present value of each named officer's accumulated pension benefits instead of their estimated annual retirement benefits. Even though retirement value varies based on an executive's circumstances under the same retirement plan, this added disclosure will likely prove eye-opening.

The pressure on limiting SERPs will increase, especially since the Pension Protection Act of 2006 will likely result in most qualified pension plans having benefits frozen and being terminated within the next 10 years (except for government, union and small, closely held companies' pension plans). As employees no longer participate in defined-benefit pension plans, SERPs, particularly those that increase benefits for executives rather than restore retirement benefits lost from qualified plans due to limits imposed by the IRS, will start to look incongruous.

Although it could be argued that a CEO's tenure has shortened over the years, the pressure of paying for performance will mount as an alternative to burdening the corporation with future costs from an underfunded SERP. Executive compensation that pays for performance is key to creating a performance culture that battles entitlement and facilitates a high-performance organization. Pfeffer also has spoken about the gap between knowing what to do and doing it—company leaders and HR champions know paying for performance is the route to follow; it is perhaps time to lead and define new best practices.

Performance Shares Lead the Way

Improved tools for determining executive compensation exist. In the future, the buck must pass to performance shares—plans that set pre-established performance levels for earning granted shares so they require more than just the tenure and "breathing" of time-based restricted stock to vest and earn long-term compensation.

Performance shares are a key strike against executive compensation programs that provide value to the executive when company performance goals may have been missed. Common measures for these shares involve absolute financial growth and relative financial performance compared to a published index of relevant companies. Time-based restricted stock is an entitlement; performance shares and performance-based restricted stock are not.

HR leaders should expect shareholders as well as boards to demand a stronger pay-for-performance relationship. They can educate executive leadership and the board of directors on long-term compensation tools, showing the different impact from time-based restricted stock compared to performance shares. Performance shares are granted to an executive contingent upon two criteria—time and results compared to measures of company performance.

If a combination of time and performance goals is achieved, the performance shares vest, and stock is transferred to the employee on a taxable basis, with a U.S. tax deduction for the company. Compensation expense is recognized over the vesting period. If the performance measure does not have market conditions (i.e., is not based on the stock price like total shareholder return), compensation expense, based on grant-date fair value, is trued up at the end and is deductible to the company based on the actual number of shares earned and awarded at the end of the period. No expense is incurred unless threshold performance is achieved under FAS123(R). Typically, upside opportunity exists for outstanding performance.

The advantage of performance shares is that the company does not have dilution from larger stock option grants with the same grant value or from issues of underwater stock options or surprises resulting from inflation in stock price that may be unrelated to company performance. Yet the executive benefits from stock-price appreciation because performance shares vest at a higher market value when stock has appreciated.

Performance shares or performance-based restricted stock will replace time-based restricted stock among companies that have gotten the message about paying for performance. And the pay-for-performance linkage will continue to strengthen in annual cash incentives as companies improve and refine measurement to include not only financial and operational measures, but also measures that strengthen the relationships between the company and both its customers and its workforce— as well as forward-focused measures that position the company for long-term success.

HR Leader's Advising Role

Most CEOs and the HR leaders who advise them on rewards want to do the right and fair thing for all concerned. Laws or regulations are unlikely to change the minority who might want to do wrong by their companies, shareholders, customers and workforce. In a "free-agency economy," we assume that if HR leaders are asked to do something inconsistent with a basic code of conduct, they should and will move on to better things. The best consultants do this, and we believe top HR leaders have more important issues than to worry about paying CEOs more than is justified. The time is now for HR leaders to step up to the plate.

Executive compensation is controversial regardless of what you do, but becomes a lightning rod when executives win and the company, shareholders, workforce and customers lose. Studies show that companies that pay for performance outperform those that do not. HR leaders must take a stronger role in guiding and educating the executive team on executive compensation direction and its impact on the rest of the organization and other interested parties. Addressing the following is a start:

- Is executive compensation aligned with the long-term health and success of the company?
- Are performance levels calibrated appropriately to levels of executive compensation?
- Is executive compensation sending messages that conflict with the messages sent to the workforce on compensation?
- Are messages about executive compensation aligned with performance initiatives that executives are sponsoring and championing throughout the organization?
- Are the board and the board's HR committee connected with the messages about compensation that the rest of the workforce gets?
- What would employees think of the executive compensation program?

Executive compensation tools, measures and messages need to be under the microscope and viewed from the standpoint of reasonableness and governance. With more understandable disclosure, compensation and performance should be put in line so you are proud of the current executive compensation in your company and do not need to fear what employees and local newspapers will say about it.

The Future Is Now

In the near future, some important changes will occur in workforce rewards, including executive compensation. Enlightened self-interest of company leaders, boards and shareholder activists, as well as stakeholders such as customers and the general workforce, will make this a reality. First, top-to-bottom pay for performance will become more widespread. Next, performance shares will continue to grow in popularity for executive rewards because they have all the features true pay-for-performance tools need. Finally, entitlement will be replaced by a performance culture as the realities of competing for the high-performing 20 percent of the workforce become clearer and we understand what employees want in order to work in our companies.

This is a great time to raise the bar on executive compensation in companies where it is too low and keep it high where it is already high. In our estimation, HR leaders are up to the challenge.

Reprinted from *HR Executive*, November 2006, 20 (16), 67-69.

CHAPTER 14:

Executive Compensation within Nonprofits: Rewarding Excellence and Ensuring Governance

The fervor over excessive executive compensation has become a major issue in organizations from coast to coast. Organizations are changing executive compensation advisers, and board members are either learning more about the executive compensation programs they are asked to approve or, in some cases, "retiring" from boards to avoid the potential liability and embarrassment. The egregious for-profit examples of WorldCom and Enron demonstrate that board members may be called upon to personally pay to settle claims despite the relative protection provided to them via indemnification provisions and D&O insurance. The issue of corporate governance relating to executive compensation is critical for all organizations. It is in the mind's eye of leaders, board members, shareholders, the investment community and the business press.

This chapter provides guidance about the performance issue and how nonprofit and other tax-exempt organizations such as hospitals and charitable and social welfare organizations (collectively referred to hereafter as "nonprofits") can manage executive compensation when performance counts and intermediate sanctions are a reality. ("Intermediate sanctions" refers to the excise tax penalties associated with excess-benefit transactions. These penalties potentially apply only to those IRC 501(c)(3) and 501(c)(4) organizations described in the U.S. Code of Federal Regulation, Title 26, Section 53.4958-2(a) (or 26 C.F.R. 53.4958-2(a)) et seq. Similar excise-tax penalties apply to private foundations via IRC 4941.)

What is a nonprofit?

Tax-exempt organizations take on many different forms. Rules governing the various forms can be found in the Internal Revenue Code's Title 26, Section 501(c)(1) to 501(c)(28). A copy of this document can be obtained at www.worldatwork.org/worldatworkjournal

---

Our theme is one of the importance of the board's role in developing executive compensation solutions that make how executives are paid a "win" for all stakeholders—customers, the community, investors, contributors, sponsors, employees and executives. Organizations that honestly pay for performance outperform those that do not, so the business case for creating a high-performance executive rewards solution is solid.

Nonprofit organizations are universally interested in improving performance. While measures relating to performance differ between and among nonprofits, the search for excellence continues to be widespread. However, nonprofit organizations have been slower than other types of organizations to embrace the need to more closely align the senior executive team's rewards with the organization's performance. Often, nonprofits are concerned about the visibility and potential bad publicity regarding excessive compensation packages paid to their executives. But in addition to aligning executive performance and maintaining a positive public image, applicable organizations must now assess the compensation arrangements for certain organizational members to avoid potential federal and state regulation.

Intermediate Sanctions

The business case for changing how executive compensation is managed and designed in charitable organizations has therefore been strengthened by the Internal Revenue Service cracking down on perceived and real abuses of excessive compensation. Intermediate sanctions provide a way for the IRS to address excessive compensation without taking away a tax-exempt organization's tax exemption because of inurement or personal gain. Intermediate sanctions include excise taxes for both the disqualified person (commonly the executive but also others) and the organization manager who participated in the compensation decision (commonly board members). Taking away an organization's tax-exempt status will likely hurt the beneficiaries for whom the organization serves; intermediate sanctions penalize the responsible parties.

The penalty for the executive (disqualified person) found to have excessive compensation is to pay the excess benefit back to the organization, pay interest on the excess benefit, pay an excise tax equaling 25 percent of the excess benefit on each excess benefit transaction, and pay a 200 percent excise tax on the excess benefit if the executive has not paid within the 90-day correction period after the date the IRS mails notice of deficiency.

The Exempt Organizations Division of the IRS created new offices to focus, in part, on compensation abuses in charitable organizations. One of these offices, the Exempt

Organizations Electronic Initiatives Office (IRS EO-EIO) is responsible for acquiring data sources that will aid the IRS in more easily comparing executive compensation paid by tax-exempt organizations. The IRS also hired many additional EO specialists and examination agents in 2004 and set a target of 2,000 correspondence-type audits of the executive compensation in tax-exempt organizations by September 2005.

In June 2005, the report of the Panel on the Nonprofit Sector to the U.S. Senate Finance Committee recommended that the IRS more actively enforce its regulation of intermediate sanctions and the IRS should be provided the funds to do so. If good governance and resource management were not enough reason for boards and CEOs to accelerate the journey to become a high-performance nonprofit tax-exempt organization, the IRS is providing new impetus to taking this initiative.

One data source to demonstrate reasonable executive compensation in the for-profit and tax-exempt arenas is ERI's *Compensation Comparables Assessor and Tax-Exempt Survey*. This compensation survey product allows tax-exempt organizations to demonstrate reasonableness by using compensation data from Form 990s and Form 990PFs. Tax-exempt organizations also can compare themselves to similar for-profit companies using ERI's *Executive Compensation Assessor*. We are approaching this chapter from the standpoint of understanding how reasonable compensation is measured within nonprofits and with knowledge of what is needed to adequately retain and motivate executives within nonprofit organizations.

Consequences of Intermediate Sanctions to Board Members

Clearly, board members within charitable organizations owe fiduciary duties of care, loyalty and obedience. As part of the duty of care, the board must implement a process to prudently evaluate the overall reasonableness of executive compensation. Boards also must establish reasonable rewards that reflect the organization's performance and that are consistent with what other similar organizations would pay for a similar executive role and outcomes generated. Because the IRS is very active in the study of reasonable compensation, the likelihood of existing problems being uncovered is significantly increased. But whether or not board members face scrutiny from the state or federal government, it is critical that the incentive compensation paid to charities' executives appropriately rewards the executive based upon transparent and clearly established performance-based metrics.

Here's what active IRS enforcement means to board members.

• Board members for applicable organizations potentially face up to $10,000 in penalties for each excess-benefit transaction if they are found to have knowingly, willfully, and without reasonable cause participated in the excess-benefit transaction (according to 26 C.F.R. 53.4958-1(d)).

- Board members must take the time to become knowledgeable about executive compensation and follow an appropriate process for determining executive compensation. For example, technically, an automatic excess-benefit transaction occurs each time money or property passes to a "disqualified person" and there is an absence of written contemporaneous substantiation regarding the transaction according to the IRS EO CPE Text for FY 2004. This is true even if the economic benefit and total compensation conferred are reasonable.
- Board members, or the appointed committee of the board charged with determining compensation, must "obtain and rely" upon appropriate comparability data for purposes of establishing the rebuttable presumption of reasonableness for the underlying compensation arrangement (according to 26 C.F.R. 53.4958-6(c)(2)).

The rebuttable presumption (as explained in 26 C.F.R. 53.4958-6) is the organization's proactive response to the IRS' claim that compensation is excessive to shift the burden to the IRS to show that the compensation is excessive. The burden of challenging the compensation comparability data shifts to the IRS if the board follows an appropriate process to make executive compensation decisions, obtains and relies upon appropriate comparability data, and possesses a minimal amount of knowledge and expertise about executive compensation. A reasonableness opinion from an appropriate qualified, independent professional makes the rebuttable presumption even stronger.

Unlike reasonable compensation cases in the for-profit arena, and according to 26 C.F.R. 53.4958-1(d), intermediate sanctions involve potentially significant personal liability for both the disqualified person receiving the excess benefit as well as the organizational manager who allowed it to happen.

According to 26 C.F.R. 53.4958-6(c)(2), to establish the rebuttable presumption of reasonableness, among other requirements, the committee of the board charged with establishing the compensation package for the executive must not only obtain and rely upon appropriate comparability data but they must also possess a minimal amount of knowledge and expertise to properly interpret the data.

The consequences for board members serving on applicable organizations are stronger than in the for-profit sector regarding IRS regulation. IRS reasonable compensation determinations in the for-profit arena typically involve issues relating to "disguised dividends" of corporate profits. In such cases, there are no statutory tax penalties for the board members and management that approve the issuance of the compensation that is not found reasonable. Contrast this with the penalties associated with intermediate sanctions (see: 26 C.F.R. 53.4958-1(d)) and it is easy to see that corporate governance of charitable organizations can be a much more serious proposition.

Involvement of States in Reasonable Compensation for Nonprofits

In addition to the IRS, state regulatory agencies are becoming more involved. *California's Nonprofit Integrity Act* of 2004 requires that the board must review and approve compensation of the CEO/president and CFO/treasurer of California nonprofits to ensure payment is "just and reasonable." New York's Not-For-Profit Law requires that executive compensation paid be "reasonable and commensurate with the personal services provided." The Charities Division of the Minnesota Attorney General's Office in a case involving the organization HealthPartners, suggests that boards have the fiduciary duty to set reasonable compensation for services rendered and not permit unreasonable levels of compensation. (The Attorney General's report can be viewed at www.ag.state.mn.us/consumer/health/Law_Legis.htm.) Minnesota's business compliance reviews of executive compensation focus on flawed methodology and disengagement of the board. Therefore, applicable organizations must be wary of state law and regulators as well.

Reasons for Paying for Performance

In many instances organizations have statements of the intent to "pay for performance." However, many are more likely to pay based on length of service than upon actually measured differences in performance. Experience suggests, however, that organizations that pay for performance consistently outperform those that pay only for service. So the business case for creating a high-performance culture is powerful. The reasons for paying for performance in addition to complying with intermediate sanctions are to:

- **Reinforce the organization's mission, vision and goals.** Often nonprofits have statements of mission, vision, and goals that are worded in terms that do not translate into metrics that can measure executive performance. The test of the viability of vision, mission, and goals is the board's ability to define these in terms that can be used to develop performance metrics for executive compensation. So governance comes from a mission statement that can be measured in terms of accomplishment in the short and longer term.

- **Align the executive's success with the organization's success.** High-performance organizations recognize and reward success. As the organization achieves goals, the executive team should be rewarded. Executives should be paid more in years when the organization meets or exceeds goals than in years when goals are missed. It gives credibility to the goal-setting process and attracts executives who believe that their economic success and that of the organization and board they serve are closely associated.
- **Enable the organization to attract and retain executive talent.** Executives who are willing to have the board evaluate their performance will seek organizations that reward performance. Boards that are interested in executive compensation programs that reward performance will establish an executive compensation strategy and associated rewards for the executive team and then seek executives who fit the mode of helping create and sustain a performance culture. Executives who are role models of paying for performance will establish similar programs for all employees. Thus the goals of the organization become part of the job of everyone in the organization.
- **Provide a vehicle to discuss the organization's goals and progress in achieving goals.** Performance management is a key communication tool when associated with a viable program of paying for performance. The board's role is to coach and facilitate chief executive performance by periodic and objective performance reviews. At this time performance is evaluated against established goals. Where room for improvement is noted, this becomes part of the board's counseling and coaching process to make sure goals are consistently achieved and that performance is recognized and rewarded accordingly.

Protecting Tax-Exempt Boards and Organizations

Effective governance of the executive compensation program for nonprofits is clearly the answer to resolving the pay-for-performance problem. Following a normal business-focused process in order that compensation varies with the organization's performance based on concrete and pre-established metrics is a key way boards can add value to the organization and protect it and themselves from embarrassment. At a minimum, the process should include the following steps:

- Select the metrics of organizational performance best reflecting the executive team's responsibilities for the success and future of the organization.
- Consistently evaluate the executive's performance based on these clearly defined metrics of organizational performance.

- Develop executive rewards that compensate based on transparent, clearly established and predetermined changes in these metrics. Executives should earn more when the organization meets goals and less when it does not. HealthPartners represents an important example of the pitfalls associated with rewarding executives who fall short of predetermined goals. Moreover, the board must stick to these predetermined guidelines.
- Include regular review of the compensation arrangement to avoid excess-benefit transactions. Particularly, review any contracts that seek to take advantage of the "initial contract exception" to determine if the contract has been materially modified or enhanced or if the executive has failed to substantially perform her contractual obligations. If an applicable 501(c)(3) hires a new CEO with no connection to the organization, then the initial compensation arrangement paid to her may not have to satisfy this test. However, the compensation arrangement must be clearly defined and followed; otherwise the organization may run afoul of the regulations later on, should there be a material modification to the agreement (e.g., a large bonus paid out contrary to a clearly defined formula).
- Carefully review the compensation arrangement not only with the executive but also with all board members outside of the committee charged with forming the compensation package. While a subcommittee is allowed to establish the rebuttable presumption of reasonableness per the Treasury Regulations (26 C.F.R. 53.4958-6(c)(1)), each board member should be brought up to speed as to why an executive is being paid what she is being paid.
- Ensure compensation reasonableness by using data sources that the IRS will accept as appropriate and include unbiased measures of competitive compensation.

The issue of defining the compensation opportunity is an objective one. It is the platform for paying for executive performance and provides the baseline from which executive compensation is established. Each board, or designated committee, should at the very least, measure compensation reasonableness as follows.

- Define the competitive market and the market value of the job using a source of information that does not create a conflict of interest and is completely independent of bias or conflict toward organization management and the organization's auditors.
- Consistently apply the compensation data from the independent source to determine the competitive worth of the executive jobs in question. Make compensation decisions based on unbiased data that can be defended to the state or federal regulator if the compensation arrangement is brought into question.

- Use an independent "appropriate professional," as defined in 26 C.F.R. 53.4958-1(d)(4)(iii), to recommend compensation levels and systematically follow these recommendations.
- Have the independent compensation professional compare each facet of executive compensation to the competitive market. Review total compensation, cash compensation, deferred compensation, benefits, perquisites, allowances and all forms of executive compensation to be paid now or in the future. Require the independent compensation professional to provide data that includes at least the following:
  - Compensation levels paid by similarly situated organizations, taxable and non-taxable, for functionally comparable positions
  - The availability of similar services in the geographic area of the applicable tax-exempt organization
  - Current compensation surveys compiled by independent firms.

According to 26 C.F.R. 53-4958-6(c)(2)(i), the IRS considers these factors when analyzing comparability data:

- Whether a reputable firm having knowledge and expertise in the same industry as the applicable organization provided the information.
- Whether the firm was independent of both the organization and the executives whose compensation is in question.
- Whether the survey covered the period subject to the IRS examination.
- Whether the organizations surveyed were similar.
- Whether the positions considered in the surveys were comparable and
- The number of compensation surveys and the number of different organization the firms included in their surveys.

Example of Intermediate Sanctions

The IRS recently published a technical advice memoranda (TAM) providing an example of intermediate sanctions penalties imposed on a nonprofit health-care group. It is TAM 200244028. Although TAMs describe only a specific, unidentified taxpayer's situation and cannot be used or cited as precedent, the TAM is certainly informative.

In the situation at issue, the IRS imposed excise tax penalties on the CEO and the wife of a health-care group for the CEO's employment contract and post-employment "consulting agreement." In seeking to establish the rebuttable presumption, the three-step procedure that shifts the burden to the IRS to rebut the probative weight of the comparability data (26 C.F.R 53.4958(6)(b)), the health-care group retained the services of an executive compensation consulting firm and delegated the decision making to the board's personnel committee.

The IRS determined that the personnel committee failed to establish the rebuttable presumption because: (1) the comparability data was analyzed subsequent to the approval of the compensation arrangement; (2) the board minutes failed to reflect the compensation report prepared by the executive compensation consulting firm or other relevant data and (3) the personnel committee failed to establish that they possessed particular knowledge or expertise relating to the compensation paid.

The memo's implications are startling with regard to the exacting compliance that the IRS demands with regard to intermediate sanctions. The memo implies that even if a properly delegated board subcommittee properly retains the services of a qualified compensation consultant who properly prepares a timely, comprehensive comparability report, the board may still fail to establish the second step of the rebuttable presumption of reasonableness unless the board provides some evidence that they possess sufficient knowledge and expertise that will render them capable of reasonably assessing the comparability data in question.

Here, the board's assumption regarding pay for performance was made on a "bedrock of sand" rather than of substance. The total compensation was viewed as excessive, and the board came short of establishing a valid method for determining executive compensation.

Example of Paying for Performance with Reasonable Compensation at a Hospital

The hospital's objective is to pay for performance and pay reasonable compensation. It compensates executives based on a combination of the labor market plus performance. With the aid of an outside independent compensation professional, it uses the average as its competitive compensation position in the labor market for similar organizations.

Performance metrics and goals cascade from the organization's mission, vision, and business plan. Some metrics are qualitative and others are quantitative, but all are documented and measurable. Metrics include patient satisfaction, quality of care, cost management and excess of revenue over expenses. The board evaluates the CEO annually based on goal achievement and also approves new goals on an annual basis.

Base pay adjustments are primarily based on market, provided performance expectations are met and living the organization's values and competencies are demonstrated.

Performance is rewarded through a variable pay plan that still provides reasonable compensation if all goals are achieved (average total cash compensation in the labor market) and if stretch goals are all significantly exceeded (around 1 standard deviation above average). This enables pay to vary based on performance without increasing fixed pay costs. Over time, the organization refined its goal-setting process to ensure alignment of the organization and executives in executive compensation.

Conclusions and Suggestions

What should an organization do to protect itself? Here are the three critical steps.

- The compensation committee should be educated about executive compensation and its responsibilities under IRS regulation and, if applicable, state regulation. It should decide on a process for determining executive compensation. Ignorance is no longer an alternative.
- The organization should require a competitive compensation analysis and written opinion by an appropriate qualified independent professional. Compensation is considered reasonable if the amount paid is what would be ordinarily paid for like services (duties and responsibilities) by like organizations (industry, size, nature) under like circumstances (location). Consideration can be given to the individual's special skills and experience, the particular nature of the individual's duties and nature of the individual, the amount of time the individual devotes to the position, and measurable performance.
- The compensation committee should make an informed decision on reasonable executive compensation, document the decision adequately, and approve it in advance of payment. There should be no conflict of interest. The compensation committee must make a reasonable attempt to ascertain if compensation is excessive and must act if it is aware of an excess benefit transaction. Silence or inaction is not viable—the board member must dissent on the record regarding excessive compensation.

This is just exercising good business judgment. It is the job of the board of nonprofits, as it is in all organizations, to establish executive compensation programs that are reasonable, competitive and reward executive performance. The U.S. Congress for one believes this is not the case in many nonprofits because it passed IRC 4958 and has determined to set this right in the short and longer term. Where does your executive compensation program stand compared to objective measures of reasonableness under intermediate sanctions? If the IRS challenges your organization's compensation determination, what will it find?

Corporate governance is an important issue. Because of the visible and public nature of many nonprofits, it is important to diagnose your board and organizational liability and vulnerability relative to pay for performance under intermediate sanctions. It may be too late when the IRS is at the door asking questions you are unable to answer. But the timing may be right to review all executive compensation practices as early as practicable.

First published in *WorldatWork Journal*, Fourth Quarter 2005, 14 (4), 62-71.

Pay for Performance Works: The U.S. Postal Service Presents a Powerful Business Case

T he U.S. Postal Service (USPS) has reached an important milestone—10 years of a fully integrated and successful market-based and performance-driven pay strategy for 75,000 white-collar employees, ranging from supervisors to postmasters to executives and officers. The USPS pay-for-performance experience can serve as a role model not only for the federal government but also for state and local governments, nonprofits and private-sector companies.

This chapter presents concrete proof that pay for performance works, and shows how the USPS experience stacks up with success criteria applicable to any organization wishing to take on the daunting task of paying people right. The chapter is based on the USPS performance history included in the annual report, the annual Comprehensive Statement on Postal Operations and other information that is unpublished but publicly available.

Organizational Success at the USPS

In the 24 years of the USPS following the Postal Reorganization Act of 1970, the service lost $10 billion. This financial performance did not meet expectations for an organization tasked with breaking even. Something had to be done. In 1995, the USPS implemented its first fully integrated pay-for-performance program for white-collar employees. In the 10 years since 1995, the financial picture turned 180 degrees. Net income has totaled $10 billion—finally offsetting the previous 24 years of net losses.

The results are not confined to financial performance. Customer service, employee workplace and productivity indicators have reached record levels. Check out the USPS' 2004 annual report: " ... service in all measured categories reached record levels ... a record fifth straight year of positive total productivity ... eliminated $1.5 billion in costs ... significant increases in safety and employee satisfaction." During the 10 years of the USPS' pay-for-performance programs, the organization achieved the following significant improvements in critical performance metrics:

- On-time delivery for first-class mail quickly jumped more than 10 percentage points and is now at a record of 95 percent (Exhibit 15-1).
- Workplace safety performance has steadily improved, with illness and injury rates now at all-time lows (Exhibit 15-2).
- Productivity has increased a record five straight years and is on course to improve a sixth year (Exhibit 15-3).

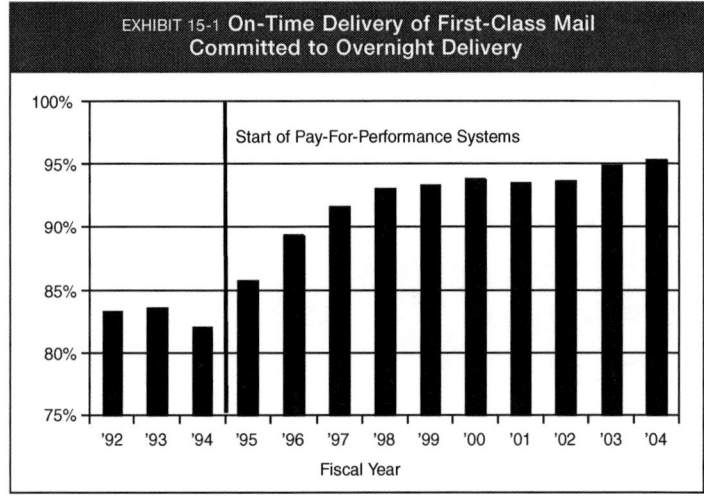

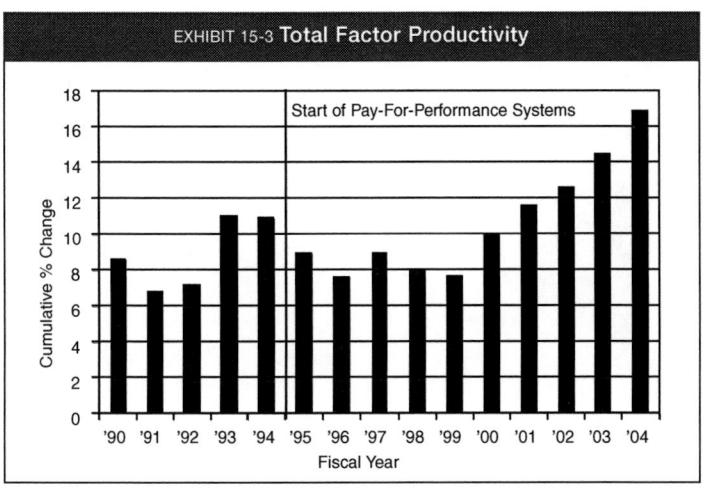

EXHIBIT 15-3 **Total Factor Productivity**

Success Criteria for Pay For Performance

With all that is written about paying for performance, considerable doubt remains among skeptics. Some critics object to pay for performance due to the absence of measurable results that would justify an organization's expenditure of time and effort. Yet, the alternative is traditionally to pay for length of service, competitive practice and the value of jobs, competence and skill. While these are important and need the attention of pay designers, organizations hire employees to help achieve organizational goals. CEOs are asking for value from the millions of dollars expended on their workforces.

The test of whether pay for performance works is the exploration of a system over time to determine if the organization is more likely to achieve its goals with pay for performance than without it. Research in the private sector suggests that when employees have a portion of their financial compensation based on concrete performance goals, these goals are more likely to be achieved than when they are not paid for performance. In the private sector, paying for performance "brands" the organization as one that is interested in attracting and retaining employees who are interested in having their performance rewarded. The practice also attracts managers who are willing and able to make the objective performance decisions necessary and be accountable for allocating the rewards they must distribute based on these performance decisions.

Research and experience suggest a pay-for-performance system does work, but commitment is required and the system is not always easy to implement and sustain. Ignoring performance as a compensation factor is easier than paying for performance. However, it just makes sense to better financially compensate those who meet goals than those who do not.

How does an organization make pay for performance work? When the following criteria exist, they make a powerful business case for success. These success criteria include:

1. Leadership champions
2. Concrete metrics
3. Meaningful reward differences
4. Communications and involvement
5. Time to make the system work.

There are more requirements for making pay for performance successful and they are worthy of discussion and exploration. However, most would agree that these five are essential, that pay for performance will not meet success without them and they are critical tests that need to be passed.

Leadership Champions

Leadership champions are senior managers who sponsor and advocate pay for performance and do so consistently and strongly over time. They are also leaders who serve as role models for the system.

The USPS was blessed with four consecutive postmaster generals who believed that a system that financially compensated employees who met goals would deliver the outcomes USPS customers deserved. If one postmaster general in the line of succession believed otherwise, the initiative would not have had the championing needed for success. The leaders realized that if they were able to get employees more effectively focused on key goals and objectives, they would be more likely to achieve these goals. Before the pay-for-performance initiative, compensation was misaligned with organizational goals. Employees were paid the same no matter what the USPS achieved. Consider the contributions of the last four postmasters general listed in Exhibit 15-4.

Concrete Metrics

Concrete metrics are goals and performance indicators that are measurable and observable, and thus can be influenced by those whose pay is impacted by changes (or lack of changes) in performance on these goals and indicators.

Under the *Five Year Strategic Plan and Annual Performance Plans*, the USPS Board of Governors reviews and approves the pay system's performance indicators and target levels of performance. Target performance levels are designed at the unit and individual levels to ensure a roll-up to national success. The overlap of objective

EXHIBIT 15-4 **Postmaster Generals Who Led Performance Reforms**

- Jack Potter (2001-present). Led the transformation of the Postal Service through the development of a new Pay-For-Performance Program with performance measures that have a clear line of sight to supervisors and postmasters. Led USPS to a record five-straight years of productivity growth.

- Bill Henderson (1998-2001): Led the continuous commitment to the economic value added (EVA) variable pay program.

- Marvin Runyon (1992-1998): Led the adoption of a new market-based and performance-driven pay system for white-collar employees.

- Anthony Frank (1988-1992): Led the development of numerous performance measures to objectively track and improve organizational performance.

performance indicators for officers, executives and middle and supervisory management ensures a common vision and sharing of organizational success.

The current USPS Pay-For-Performance Program contains 10 corporate indicators and 44 unit indicators, with different weights for 24 different job families covering 75,000 employees. In each organizational level, great care is given to assigning the proper weight to indicators that employees have an opportunity to influence. So within a given organizational unit, the top manager will have a balance of customer, workplace and business objectives, while the functional managers like finance and HR will have more weight on finance and HR indicators.

Each position has a mix of corporate, unit and individual indicators and numerical targets. Exhibit 15-5 displays performance indicators at the corporate level. Exhibit 15-6 indicates the performance indicators at the unit level and Exhibit 15-7 indicates examples of performance indicators at the individual level.

To improve the line of sight for participants, weights differ for corporate/unit/individual indicators based on a position's level in the organization. Exhibit 15-8 is a graphic illustration of this concept.

Meaningful Reward Differences

With limited pay and rewards budgets, organizations must allocate enough to rewarding performance to make it worthwhile for employees to meet the goals. Performance must be worth more than nonperformance to provide a "win-win" with the organization.

Under the USPS system, each concrete metric listed in Exhibit 15-5, Exhibit 15-6 and Exhibit 15-7 is weighted for line of sight, and 15 different performance levels. When results are assessed against these metrics and weights, an overall performance rating of 1 to 15 is provided to each employee. Exhibit 15-9 provides an illustration of the 15-point rating system.

Once the rating is determined, a straightforward link exists to a pay action as illustrated in Exhibit 15-10. Under the postal system, actions can range up to 12 percent. Actions are paid as salary increases to the maximum of the employee's pay grade, with any balance paid as a lump sum.

EXHIBIT 15-5 FY 2005 Performance Indicators at the Corporate Level		
Improve Service	Enhance Performance-Based Culture	Generate Revenue; Manage Costs
On-time delivery of ... • First-Class Overnight • First-Class Two-Day • First-Class Three-Day • Priority Mail—Surface • Priority Mail—Air • Express Mail	• OSHA Illness and Injury Rate • Employee opinion survey score	• National total revenue • Total factor productivity

EXHIBIT 15-6 FY 2005 Performance Indicators at the Unit Level		
Improve Service	Enhance Performance-Based Culture	Generate Revenue; Manage Costs
• Customer service survey score • Delivery scan rates	• Motor vehicle accident rates • Safety programs • Grievance rates • Injury comp rates	• Total operating expense • Retail revenue

EXHIBIT 15-7 Examples of FY 2005 Performance Indicators at the Individual Level			
Customer Services	Mail Processing	Finance	Maintenance
• Cost per delivery • Rural hours percent to standard • Letter carrier work hours • Clerk work hours	• Work hours • Throughput • Delivery confirmation scanning • Cancellations rates	• Total operating expense performance to plan • Segmented Inventory Accountability (SIA) • Statistical programs	• Preventative maintenance and bypass rate • Equipment availability • Jams per 10K • Labor cost per 1,000 pieces

Have there been meaningful distinctions in performance in the Postal Service experience? For fiscal year 2004, the overall national performance score was 9 on the 15-point scale, and unsurprisingly, the median performance rating for 75,000 employees was also 9. A bell curve around the median rating showed employees equally likely to get ratings above and below the median. The range of ratings was 3 to 14, and when combined with a foundation of objective performance metrics, provides concrete evidence that meaningful distinctions in performance have been made.

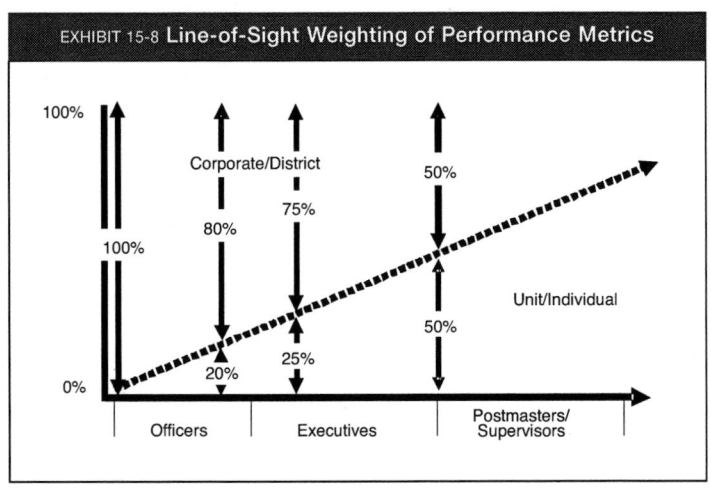

EXHIBIT 15-8 **Line-of-Sight Weighting of Performance Metrics**

Noncontributor	Contributor		High Contributor	Exceptional Contributor
EXHIBIT 15-9 **Point Rating Matrix**				
3	6	9	12	15
2	5	8	11	14
1	4	7	10	13

Noncontributor	Contributor		High Contributor	Exceptional Contributor
EXHIBIT 15-10 **Nonexecutive Pay Actions**				
0	3.5%	6.5%	9.5%	12.0%
0	3.0%	5.75%	8.75%	11.0%
0	2.5%	5.0%	8.0%	10.25%

Paid as salary increase up to grade maximum salary; balance is paid as a lump-sum payment if the award would take the individual's salary above maximum

Communications and Involvement

Like any new initiative, a process is needed for moving to pay for performance that includes involving those impacted by the change. A strong logic for the need for change is required. What the change means to those involved needs to be consistently communicated for those involved in making the changes and those impacted.

Opportunities for leaders to communicate the reasons for change and involving people in the change process have a solid foundation in the USPS. The USPS has unique institutions called "management associations." These associations are recognized under the Postal Reorganization Act of 1970. There are three management associations representing approximately 60,000 supervisors and postmasters across the United States. The law calls for a regular schedule of program consultations and periodic pay consultations. Through the management associations, the USPS organized focus groups of supervisors and postmasters to develop individual, objective performance indicators that were common to their positions. These individual-level indicators supplemented and supported the corporate and unit-level indicators under the new Pay-For-Performance Program. The Postal Service's success in reforming its pay programs and achieving a performance-based culture is largely due to the positive relationship with the management associations.

During the last 10 years, the USPS used a variety of written, audio-visual and face-to-face techniques to communicate compensation and performance issues with employees. Written communications include the written pay package with the management associations, letters to employees, employee brochures and management and association periodicals. Audio-visual communications include live satellite television training, extensive use of Web resources and recorded CD/DVDs. Face-to-face communications include special and regularly scheduled management conferences and association conferences. For example, in 2003 an HR conference of 300 people, including officials of the management associations, initiated the new Pay-For-Performance Program.

Performance indicators under the USPS Pay-For-Performance Program are posted on the internal Web site that contains descriptions of how the indicator is measured, defines 15 different target levels for each performance indicator and describes how employees can improve performance on the indicator. Monthly status reports on each performance indicator are published on the internal Web site so that everyone in the organization can see how progress is being made toward target performance levels. The Web site is also used for submitting individual ratings to higher management levels for review and approval.

Most methods of communications were applied during the program's 10 years to ensure that everyone received and understood the message that (1) performance was tied to income, (2) the compensation system was necessary for the USPS' success and (3) employees are critical stakeholders in that success.

Time to Make the System Work

There must be a long-term commitment to make change and "stay the course." There must be a consistency of effort even though there is a change in "how it is done here." Patience and the willingness to repeat the message build trust and understanding.

The history of performance-driven pay at the USPS illustrates this point. The USPS pay-for-performance started in 1991 with the implementation of a modest group-incentive program titled "Striving For Excellence Together" (SET). The SET Program provided small lump-sum payments for success on a limited number of performance measures. However, during the four years of SET, annual general increases, biannual cost-of-living adjustments and step increases defined white-collar salary increases.

In 1995, the white-collar system was reformed to include a larger group-incentive program with a balanced scorecard of performance measures, and a merit pay program for providing one annual salary increase based on individual performance. The group-incentive program was the Economic Value Added (EVA) Variable Pay Program. The Merit Pay Program continued to be focused on individual performance, but with only three ratings options—far exceeded objectives, met objectives and unacceptable. These two programs created organizational success for seven years.

Like any organization seeking cultural change, USPS experienced bumps along the road. Because the EVA Variable Pay Program was a complex and often-misunderstood financial performance measure, especially in a break-even environment, it became necessary to replace it. At the same time, the Merit Pay Program came under scrutiny for its limited ability to make meaningful performance distinctions. Therefore, the USPS transitioned to a new Pay-For-Performance Program in 2003 without abandoning its market-based, performance-driven principles. The new Pay-For-Performance Program improved accountability for individual contributions to organizational success; provided clear expectations and feedback on progress toward goals; and rewarded exceptional individual performance for achieving challenging objectives. Through a variety of challenges, the USPS stayed the course.

USPS: The Business Case Shows Success

In the last 10 years, the USPS implemented pay for performance for the management and professional workforce—a sole change improving measurable performance and customer satisfaction to an extent that it could be an example for companies in the for-profit sector. The USPS migration to the system meets all five critical challenges that a viable system must meet.

Does tying financial compensation to performance really work? If "work" is defined in terms of improving an organization's proven ability to achieve critical goals and objectives and do so on a consistent basis, then the answer from the USPS' performance results is a resounding "yes, and we have the results to prove it." How often has an organization moved from a culture where employees are given cost-of-living adjustments to one where the organization is seeking new performance metrics as a result of coming so close to achieving maximum goal performance with superior results on existing organizational performance standards? Seldom or never is the most probable answer in most cases.

The major change at USPS was to compensate nonunion professional and management employees by paying for performance. Pay for performance accelerated the commitment to organizational success at USPS. It was built around the most important performance priorities. While market-based, performance-driven compensation at the USPS is 10 years old, the implementation of the new Pay-For-Performance Program allowed the USPS to achieve higher levels of breakthrough performance during the last two years.

Fiscal Year 2005 saw the completion of the 11th year of the USPS' pay-for-performance initiative. As discussed in the *Federal Times*, "Overall, it was a very good year. Our service levels are solid, and we have reduced the injury and illness rate. In financial terms, our productivity was up 1.1 percent last year, the sixth straight year of a productivity increase." The headline said it all, "2005: Financially, USPS' best year since '70s."

This is a case study in success. The USPS is one of the most exciting performance cultures in the United States and across the globe. Pay for performance works, and the USPS' track record is proof. If the USPS, with 75,000 employees and operating with a history of losses, can achieve success, consider what organizations in the nonprofit and for-profit sectors can do. With a handful of success criteria as a guide, organizations can create wonders for their stakeholders.

First published in *WorldatWork Journal*, First Quarter 2006, 15 (1), 24-31.

CHAPTER 16

Evaluating Human Resource Pay and Rewards Computer and Web Products

For years the management of pay and rewards has been weakly supported from the systems and applications standpoint. In fact, for years the support came from either spreadsheets or central computer services. However, computer and Web-based solutions abound. Organizations have a host of alternatives available that offer ways to accelerate and simplify the administration and communication of pay and rewards information. But what potential value do these solutions add to businesses?

What's needed to permit a more complete opportunity to streamline pay and rewards management? Utility and value for the cost and complexity of shopping for a system that meets an organization's needs, implementing the system in the organization and communicating and training in how to get the most from the system is the answer. The application of technology to pay and rewards is a critical priority, and the resources are available to make it a reality.

Infrastructure and Substance

Probably the most significant innovation in the pay and rewards arena in the past 50 years was the point-factor plan, invented decades ago by Ned Hay. This solution had an infrastructure for pay management in the form of jobs having various point values based on their worth to the organization. It also was a substantive solution because it provided logic of job values that helped the organization determine why and how jobs differ in value to the organization. The solution provided a foundation for job valuing and managing pay.

The organization would value jobs based on factors such as knowledge require-ments and management responsibilities. This value was translated into numerical scores. The jobs with high scores were worth more to the organization than those with low scores. And the employees in these jobs had base pay opportunities deter-mined by how many points their job was worth. Because many organizations used the same solution, it became a powerful and universal way to determine the value of jobs in an organization. And it was the way to exchange information with other organizations, because it became a standard of comparison. It was universally appli-cable and received considerable support. It worked because it was substance plus infrastructure. It may be obsolete now, but there has not been an equally successful replacement program for valuing jobs.

Needs for the Next Decade

The call is for agile solutions that can adapt as needed. The focus on flexibility is important and essential, especially for pay and rewards designs, because they communicate business directions. They are also what are called sources of "hot" change for organizations—when changes are made to pay and rewards, they affect everyone included in the change and do so quickly.

The alternative to pay and rewards change is "cold" change. For example, new recruitment and selection initiatives are slow to influence the organization and then may only affect employees who are not yet organization members. This is a very important distinction to make that places great value on change communi-cated through pay and rewards. And to magnify the importance of the issue, pay and rewards are often one of the top one or two opportunity costs that organiza-tions are able to manage to get the most business value from creating a positive relationship with all employees.

Organizations often seem more willing to initiate many other changes but hesitate in changing pay and rewards. So when they finally do make this important decision, change must be implemented properly the first time around. Pay change failures have a lasting negative impact on organizations and employees. And they make doing it the second time around extremely hard because considerable damage to the trust bond between organizations and employees can result from failure.

Computer-based pay management systems and Internet applications can support pay and rewards programs and policies by simplifying and accelerating pay management. The use of technology to replace even the most sophisticated manual solutions is needed and inevitable.

Selecting Products

All the major pay and rewards conferences and most HR conferences of note have extensive exhibit halls that are available to vendors who market their wares to conference attendees. Conference exhibits are one of the best opportunities for organizations to compare and contrast the alternative products, based on their needs and what vendors have to offer.

It is best to begin by putting together a list of the features and capabilities your organization needs relative to computer-based and/or Web-based tools. What are the five most important things a system can provide to your organization? What is your wish list? What questions do you want potential vendors to answer to give you and your organization assurance that they can deliver to your business? What do you need to know beyond the demonstration that will help you and your organization make the right selection? What feedback can you provide to the vendors offering products and services that can help them deliver a solution that meets the needs of your organization?

The advantages these products provide include the following:

- **Recordkeeping.** They all provide a streamlined and understandable way to manage the data needed to administer pay and rewards programs. They keep records and integrate with the organization's data processing and systems capability.
- **Management of costs.** The solutions permit the active management of pay and rewards budgets based on predetermined parameters. They allow tracking expenses and evaluating the relationship between goal and metric performance and costs incurred.
- **Administrative ease.** They facilitate administration and ease access to the substance of the programs, increasing the speed with which all pay and rewards programs can be managed. And they permit management of these programs by nonexpert personnel.
- **Communications.** Graphic capability permits frequent communication of progress to goal performance to be monitored and presented. Participants can receive periodic updates and information on "where we are" and also "where we need to go," relative to metrics and objectives.
- **Reports and analysis.** Data analysis and report preparation are facilitated and accelerated. Information can be disaggregated in a customized fashion to meet a variety of needs. And the speed of access is much quicker than without such systems.

- **Forms and formats.** The systems provide ways to organize the information and ways to manage it from a computer terminal. They display the information in a businesslike fashion and permit comparisons and updates and standard ways for employees and managers to look at the information. They are standardized, which helps with training on program workings and facilitates continuous improvement.
- **Improved accuracy.** The systems universally ensure a level of accuracy that is not possible otherwise. They directly utilize the information available on the organization's general HR information system, substantially improving quality control of information and providing checks and balances.

However, these systems also have some shortcomings that may or may not be critical. Some of these possible problems include the following:

- **Lack of uniqueness.** Seemingly, the systems lack differentiation. If one is able to gain a unique feature that others do not have, the others will copy them as soon as the programmers can get back to work.
- **Absence of better practice.** All of the systems are essentially "value free" and use this feature as a selling point. All say that their system can accept any programs and policies the organization wishes to implement and use. Instead of creating the opportunity to improve existing practice, these systems reinforce existing practice, no matter how well aligned it is with organizational goals.
- **Acceleration of goal mismatches.** When existing practice is reinforced with an automated pay and rewards solution, the focus is more on making the system work rather than on approving policy and practice to better communicate the key goals and priorities of the organization. If goals and metrics do not match current needs, then they often do not change during the transition to the new system solution.
- **Lack of critique capability.** The systems are designed to reinforce existing practice, and no capability exists by means of the system to apply evaluative criteria to judge the extent to which the substance of pay and rewards programs meet the ever changing needs and goals of the organization. Capability does not exist to evaluate the "rightness" of plans and programs to match the strategy and objectives of pay and rewards to the needs of the organization and relate this information to prevailing practice or to however the system might define best practice.
- **Infrastructure only.** The systems provide value-free architecture but not content. And the organizations marketing these systems promote this feature as a positive factor. However, this often merely propagates an unaligned pay and rewards solution.

- **Unstable provider sample.** With a few exceptions, the vendors change nearly annually. A few years ago, some 30 vendors were selling 360-degree performance management products that were computer supported. Now, very few offer such products. Every trip through the vendor products arena for pay and rewards products finds fewer and different vendors. Only the largest of the providers continues to exist from year to year. The provider base is not secure, and an organization may buy from a vendor who will not be there to service the purchase.
- **Complexity.** Because the systems make administration more streamlined and quicker, it is possible to implement a highly complex underlying pay and rewards program. When systems are more difficult to administer, the tendency is to clarify and simplify the design and the communication messages delivered. The systems make it possible to manage pay and rewards without simplifying the messages or the metrics and goals.

The problem is not that these solutions do not add value to the organizations that use them. It is just that they have not made the powerful "value to the business" leap that seems within their reach.

The Next Decade

Two key tasks must be completed to make these products more valuable. First, new product and service development needs to focus more on determining and responding to client or potential client needs rather than on merely copying tools from competitors. In addition, these products need to offer substance in addition to infrastructure. Most vendors claim that they do not provide substance because users can implement any program and the system will permit them to include and manage it. They suggest that customers want to have the system manage their existing pay and rewards solution, not require a different solution. The best way to address this issue would be to provide the user the opportunity to use a best practice pay and rewards solution that can be selected from alternatives imbedded in the system as an alternative to the existing system.

First published in *Compensation & Benefits Review*, September/October 2005, 37 (5), 42-45. Reprinted by permission of SAGE Publications Inc.

PART V
Moving Forward

CHAPTER 17:
Pay Changes Going Forward

Where are pay strategies and practices headed? During the late 1990s, we saw an aggressive people buildup in a scarce-talent business environment, resulting in more generous pay and benefits and a strong emphasis on competitive total pay. Then early in this century, global recession hit and staffing momentum diminished, with major employee reductions, pay and benefit cuts and eventually a return to workforce disenfranchisement. This wrenching HR change occurred within a short period and continues to affect pay practices. Our goal here is to predict what might be in store for total pay in the next few years based on an understanding of what has occurred in total pay over the past two decades and knowledge of total pay practices of prior "into-out-of" recession and economic growth periods.

Realities Come Home to Roost

We have seen some significant changes that were forced on companies relative to management of total pay. Companies that do not heed the implications of and communicate about the changing economic scene will send mixed messages to their workforce. Lack of communication and consistency is a major reason it is so hard to get people to align themselves and to consistently endeavor to do what is necessary to help the business be a success. The wrenching of total pay design during the past 20 years can be summarized as follows:

- **Entitlement period.** Most of the history of pay involves entitlement disguised as a nearly singular emphasis on internal equity. It emphasized internal job relationships more than what the external market paid for jobs and the skills people needed to perform the jobs. Companies purchased job evaluation systems that assigned points for the job features that companies believed could determine what a job was worth—so many points for "knowledge" and so many for "management," for example.

  The consequence of this entitlement period was to value jobs that had different market values but perceived similar internal values about the same. This caused many companies to underpay people in jobs with higher-market values and overpay jobs with lower-market values. When companies are in a short-supply situation relative to skills that have a high market value, they must either ignore internal valuing or hire in the aftermarket relative to talent-seeking employees that other companies do not want to hire. Internal equity also overpays people who have less market-worthy skills and thereby encourages them to ignore opportunities to acquire and apply skills that justify higher compensation levels.

- **Reengineering and rightsizing period.** For a host of reasons, including the internal focus on job valuing, companies grew taller and broader in terms of organizational design. Multiple levels and layers created communication challenges and perhaps excessive HR costs, plus duplication of efforts and lack of clear accountability and responsibility. For a number of reasons, a score of reengineering and rightsizing initiatives hit global business, and this resulted in a "slash and burn" mentality relative to workforce cutbacks. Companies became leaner and shorter, and many people who had counted on spending a full career with one company were on the street.

The only positive workforce result from this was the end of point-factor and internal-equity pay systems in all but the most bureaucratic and tenure-focused companies. People received pay cuts and pay freezes and began to hear about "pay at risk," and some companies began to push incentives and variable pay lower in the organization and re-emphasize the pay-for-performance concept. The problem with all of this was company leadership and workforce readiness for change—people were not ready to accept pay changes. Consequently, confusion reigned, and pay solutions were seldom well aligned with the business messages the company intended to deliver through pay and rewards design.

- **The new workforce deal period.** Major realignment resulted in what is often called the "new deal"—where employees had to learn new ways of behaving and also realize that they would likely not spend an entire career with one company. Free agency became popular, and employees learned that periods of unemployment or necessary self-employment would be part of a working career. Employees had to go more than half way to work for a company with dynamic and changing work needs. Paying for skill acquisition and application received attention. Also, paying for competencies became an alternative answer to paying for jobs. But skill pay and competency pay struggled for lack of practicality and a strong business case for changing pay. Positive results from this period included strong experimentation in the areas of paying for what people do in value-added terms rather than just for the inanimate jobs they hold. This gave more credibility to the idea that people and not jobs are what add value to the business. Also, broader use of incentives and variable pay was a positive legacy from this period. The use of business metrics for incentives became more important. How performance was to be measured in the future became a part of pay design. This period had considerable momentum, but as in the past, business changes created a "time out" in pay change.

- **Scarce talent and "best places to work" period.** In the mid-1990s, a global business boom and a swelling technology sector placed a premium not only on technical stills but also on workers in general. Although all the elements of total rewards were brought into active play, the focus was on the total pay arena—more base pay, incentives, benefits and recognition and celebration. The purely financial elements of rewards were used as the primary lever to get and keep the people the companies needed to fill their many slots. Also, best-place-to-work branding opportunities became valued "clubs" to join. Companies believed their job-filling cases were strengthened by providing extremely liberal benefits without a win-win for both the company and workforce—unless just getting the employee to remain with the company could be considered the win for the company.

    The jury is out about if becoming a best place to work adds value to the company's business in the longer term. This is because the criteria for being picked as a best place by either *Fortune* or *Working Mother* do not include creating a link between the company providing the added benefits in exchange for improved value the employees can provide. This could be better performance or productivity, improved quality and customer care or the acquisition and application of some needed skill the company believes is critical to the business. Also, many companies made job-security pledges and promises of sabbaticals that became liabilities when times turned bad or when employees with tenure proved unwilling or unable to learn or perform up to what they were being paid.

- **The better workforce deal and total rewards.** Many companies came to realize that the best people with the most important skills work for more than just pay. The best people work for companies with a compelling future to offer, plus the chance to grow as individuals, a place that offers a positive work experience and of course total pay including base pay, benefits, incentives and recognition and celebration. These were combined into total rewards packages and customized to match specific branding objectives for the messages they most want to communicate to their workforce. The wisest of these companies make total rewards part of a deal contingent on the company maintaining some acceptable level of performance. They also include a workable performance management system that requires employee growth and a base pay solution that requires new skill and competence as a requirement for more of the total rewards package. The clear future of total rewards is in supporting the business process of the company. When the company wins, people win. Whether you build it into the total rewards solution or not is not the issue, but doing so provides an upside and a downside. If companies fail to build the performance "deal" into the rewards solution they deploy, employees only share in the downside of a business slump through layoffs, pay cuts, demotions or increased job load due to workforce reductions and often without notice. These events may happen with a win-win solution to total rewards, but the upside is there too, as is the understanding of the relationship from the beginning of the employment deal.

- **2000-2002 global recession and Sept. 11 period.** A series of emotional and economic lightning bolts hit beginning mid-2000 and continuing into 2002. Companies pulled back on a number of rewards initiatives that were in full swing—some of which had solid momentum. Although employers did not really return to the reengineering and rightsizing period, they did go back to a slash-and-burn mentality as it relates to total pay and total rewards. Because multiple calamities were in motion at the same time, there was no prevailing practice information to fall back on. The result was a return to workforce disenfranchisement and loss of trust.

- **Economic recovery.** Total rewards had the chance to regain momentum, and the opportunity for reinvention returned. Companies that did not demolish their rewards solution during the recession could build their new directions as a continuation of their commitment to a long-term, thick-and-thin times rewards strategy that works for their company. But those companies that did not keep the course during the recession had an opportunity to revitalize rewards to improve and renew the business message the workforce needed to hear.

- **The future.** Finally, we arrive at the challenges that face us. Some of the challenges that Jim O'Toole and Ed Lawler articulate in *The New American Workplace* include the misalignment of business needs and employee skills, "free agent" employees (those who will not spend an entire career with one organization), retiring baby boomers with critical skills and competencies, employee concerns about the balance between work and life/family, and the ineffective utilization of human capital. But opportunities are also significant. Organizations can communicate an integrated package of total rewards with a strong message about rewarding high performance because it is in everyone's best interest. Reward tools evolve. Companies may need new and more all-inclusive cash and equity-based incentives based on metrics that help accelerate business success. For some companies with a limited budget, the integration may be led by recognition and celebration initiatives that bring a rallying message to the workforce, followed by new goals for performance management. In addition, organizations will need communication that aids understanding of the workforce's importance to business success and reasonable benefits that make a company attractive to the types of employees who remain valuable in the longer term.

Predicting the Future

Exhibit 17-1 summarizes the current transformation and describes the tools we believe will help an enterprise use rewards to help it communicate its future. We have emphasized just total pay—base pay, incentives, recognition and celebration and benefits. But although these reward elements may be in the front of people's minds, companies need also to be concerned about the other total rewards components.

- **Base pay.** Because of the shortage and mismatch of skilled talent, the future rests with how effectively a company can focus the most fixed element of total pay—base pay—on growth in employee value to the business. Skill-based pay and paying for competencies are options but have struggled. Practicality and reasonable simplicity are not strong suits for existing pay solutions that profess to pay for relevant new skills and competencies that add to the worth of the company. The concept of paying for skills rather than the job makes incredible sense. But there have been too many failures caused by complexity, overdesign, haste and poor communication to simply return to these solutions without study and consideration.

  The future depends on our ability to develop and implement a base pay system with a foundation in competitive practice so that the company and the employee have a pay relationship that is anchored in the marketplace. Also, any base pay adjustments need to depend on the employee's acquiring and using the skill and competence the business needs to produce results to justify a higher base pay level. This means linking a base pay valuing system with the performance management solution. This type of pay program currently exists in portions of IBM and other major companies. However, prevailing practice continues to separate how base pay is valued and how base pay is adjusted on an individual basis.

  In the future, base pay will represent the longer-term sustained business value-added of the individual in terms of performance and skills and competence. Incentives and recognition will reward specific results.

EXHIBIT 17-1 **Workplace Total Pay: The Future**

Total Pay Component	Prediction for Future
Base Pay	Continues to be under pressure as a fixed cost of labor.
Valuing	Emphasis on value-added strategies that start with an understanding of competitive practice, but competitiveness will not be the primary/only factor in the equation.
Adjustments	Base pay increases as employees gain in and provide business value. The more skill/capability the company needs, the more base pay rises. Not every employee will be guaranteed competitive base pay without a commitment to career growth and adding business value through results.
Incentives	The future for total pay because no other tool matches their flexibility.
Metrics	Refine and combine longer with shorter line-of-sight measures and goals to balance rewarding individual, team, unit and company results.
Cash	Increase in importance as a portion of total cash compensation. Better education concerning metrics and reality that incentives do not pay when goals are missed. More focus on rewarding individual results.
Equity	Return to importance with performance-based equity (e.g., performance shares). More communications and education concerning the importance and implications of stock ownership. Better management of messages associated with stock ownership in 401(k) plans going forward.
Recognition and celebration	Continue to be important but more closely integrated with other elements of total pay. More emphasis on employee involvement in the design of solutions and fewer gimmicks that have only short-term value.
Benefits	Cost-reduction targets during the next decade as benefit costs escalate. Not repeat liberalization of fixed-benefit costs during times of scarce talent and an emphasis on "best place to work" environments.

- **Incentives.** The prediction that is most likely to be realized is a new boost in incentives and performance-based equity vehicles. The answer is more of both, with continued refinement of measures, better calibration of goals, and more communication, education and engagement of employees in achieving the goals. Measures and goals closer to employee performance and more directly within employee control will be used as the basis for incentive payments as goals become more aligned with business and the goal-setting process improves. In fact, more organizations are now using incentives to reward individual performance as salary increase budgets stall. Where it makes sense from a work standpoint, increasing individual incentives will be mixed with team, unit and companywide incentives. This will be strongly influenced by the work design—for example, the extent to which individuals are in a position to influence measurable outcomes compared to optimizing team results.

- **Recognition and celebration.** Acknowledging outcomes is essential. People want their successes and accomplishments to be recognized. This means going beyond the employee-of-the-month approach to programs that are developed and managed by employees themselves—programs that are uniquely designed for a specific company by the employees who will seek the recognition and participate in the celebration. The programs will change periodically as the needs change. They must be kept fresh and positive.

Recognition and celebration are important total rewards elements because they provide significant "bang for the reward buck" and help create a positive workplace. Their reinforcement of company values and directions further legitimizes monetary and nonmonetary recognition and celebration as part of the company rewards package.

- **Benefits.** More cost cutting is in the offing here. Benefits will surely always provide protection from much of the financial risk entailed in illness, death and disability. Benefits provide attractive work-life programs when these are in the best interest of the company and workforce. But more money will be directed to other programs that are more focused on company performance.

More choice making is in the future. Employees like customizing their own benefits and view this as an important opportunity to participate in designing their future security. The cost of benefits, without further liberalization, will increase with an aging global population, so new ways need to be found to better manage these costs. And employee communications will be critical because benefits are expensive and many employees do not understand their value. The future of flexible benefits is secure, but they have become a company tool of cost savings and play this role well. In the future, flexible benefits will also increasingly become a powerful way for employees to have the chance to engineer their own benefits, increasing their appreciation of benefits and realizing the cost they represent to the company.

The future lies in helping the workforce understand that for companies to provide attractive work, employees must add value in terms of skill and competence they acquire and apply and the results they generate from their efforts.

The future will also involve more segmentation of pay and rewards based on the type of work performed and what employees value. Superkeepers, the top 20 percent performers, must be strongly rewarded because they sustain the high-performance organization and are likely attractive to other enterprises. Superkeepers and free agents are not necessarily the same. As free agents comprise more of the current workforce, businesses will need to design pay and rewards systems that reward the value added by those individuals for contributions they made during their tenure. But the rewards must be portable (such as early vesting) so free agents can take them when they depart. One-size-fits-nobody-anymore-in-an-organization will lead to customization. The message of strongly rewarding high performance, however, must be consistent across the organization.

Conclusions

Rapid change creates the chance for some new directions. Some companies will take advantage of this opportunity, and some will miss the chance and freeze where they are, or even take some backward steps. But it is a chance for rewards designers to shine if the company's rewards solution needed for business success is not in place.

Revised October 2006; first published in *Compensation & Benefits Review*, July/August 2002, 34 (4), 48-53. Reprinted by permission of SAGE Publications Inc.

CHAPTER 18:

Career Directions for Total Rewards Professionals

The past 10 years have seen the career path of compensation and benefits professionals change directions many times, but we are probably closer to the beginning of a turbulent period than the end of it. By 2010, many predict that there will be a 10 million job gap between available and employable workers and job openings. Research shows that the 20 percent most engaged, skilled and top-performing employees generate nearly three times the results of others in the organization. These superkeeper employees are critical to the success of all organizations. Few, if any, CEOs ever say, "We've got enough top players; we need more B players because we can get by with whoever we hire."[1]

This talent-scarce work environment places a premium on employees in general and top performers with key skills—the best-skilled top performers specifically. The workplace of the future will be vastly different from what it is now, and this defines what HR will need to deliver to provide organizations that seek top talent a good shot at filling their needs. Compared with these opportunities or challenges, other factors that define the workplace of the future are a much lower priority.

The role that total rewards—compensation, benefits, recognition and other noncompensation elements that are part of the value proposition for employees—will play in addressing the talent shortage may be complex and challenging. The shepherds of designing, implementing and communicating compensation and benefits solutions and balancing and integrating total rewards solutions will be the HR professionals, present and future, who become specialists in the delivery of compensation, benefits and total rewards solutions to their organizations.

Total Rewards Professionals

We believe that compensation and benefits professionals should become total rewards professionals to provide the most value to their organizations. Total rewards include not only total pay but also individual growth, a compelling future and a positive workplace. Organizations may have different configurations of the components of total rewards, but total rewards are more than just compensation and benefits. (See Exhibit 18-1.)

The role of the total rewards professional includes monitoring, evaluating and improving the entire value proposition from both sides of the equation—what both the organization and the employees receive for value provided. The value proposition that the organization makes to its employees is the total rewards package. Compensation professionals, benefits professionals and even professionals in the combined role of compensation and benefits must take into account the entire total rewards package to perform their role effectively and balance and integrate all the elements of total rewards. They must expand their view of rewards to total rewards and take a broader perspective in applying their expertise in compensation and benefits.

EXHIBIT 18-1 Total Rewards

Individual Growth
- Investment in people
- Development and training
- Performance management
- Career enhancement

Compelling Future
- Vision and values
- Company growth and success
- Company image and reputation
- Stakeholdership
- Win-win over time

Business Results

Total Pay
- Base pay
- Variable pay (cash and stock)
- Benefits or indirect pay
- Recognition and celebration

Positive Workplace
- People focus
- Leadership
- Colleagues
- Work itself
- Involvement
- Trust and commitment
- Open communication

Source: Patricia K. Zingheim and Jay R. Schuster, *Pay People Right! Breakthrough Reward Strategies to Create Great Companies.* San Francisco. Jossey-Bass, 2000.

At the Center of HR

Much has been written about "HR champions" and how they are at the center of the connections between organizations and people. If HR professionals are at the center of what organizations are about, total rewards professionals should be the core of HR. The largest opportunity costs organizations have are those dedicated to compensation and benefits for the workforce. And total rewards professionals are chartered to provide the organization with advice concerning strategy, tactics, communications, and administration of these significant expenses.

No other aspect of the HR profession has more influence on the overall budget of the organization. Through performance management, total rewards professionals communicate and translate key organizational goals to employees. How total rewards are delivered "brands" the organization to the workforce—giving clear messages to prospective and current employees about what it is like to work in the organization and defining the win-win relationship between the organization and its talent. This is a critical responsibility for HR, especially during times of scarce talent.

The problem, of course, is that when it comes to choosing a senior leader for the HR organization, this role is more likely to go to someone from a discipline other than compensation and benefits—such as employee relations, training, development, labor relations or recruitment. These are critical roles that add major value to a business but not to the exclusion of what total rewards professionals can and do contribute. We believe that part of the reason compensation and benefits leaders are overlooked is because they have not broadened themselves as total rewards leaders.

Total rewards professionals have considerable financial impact on organizations. They should have as good or better of a chance to head up the organization that is responsible for programs that manage the organization's critical asset—talent. This is certainly not a uniquely parochial view of career paths. Professional organizations in the training, development, labor relations, recruitment and other HR disciplines advocate their members for HR career growth. It is time for the associations that depend on compensation, benefits and total rewards professionals to do the same.

Call for Collaboration

Anyone who follows the literature in the compensation and benefits field that both types of professionals share will notice that very few articles address compensation and benefits from a strategic perspective. And very seldom are compensation and benefits professionals addressed together from a career perspective. Professional training designations are either in benefits or in compensation.

In a total rewards world, this no longer makes sense. Although some tactical articles include both compensation and benefits, they are often strongly focused on the challenge of managing benefits costs and at the same time keeping pay competitive in an increasingly difficult talent market. Articles that are focused on total rewards are primarily written by those in the compensation and not the benefits side of the total rewards professionals' ledger.

The reality has been that two different career paths have existed in the compensation and benefits business—one for those involved in benefits and another for those involved in compensation. And although eventually roles combine and one professional may become responsible for compensation and benefits, the career path has most commonly been quite unbalanced with the professional assuming the overall responsibility from a career in either benefits or compensation management.

The concept of total rewards is in fact a product of those principally from compensation and other rewards career paths and not from benefits management. If you sort out the alternatives that exist relative to total rewards, the ideas are rich in content relative to compensation and other nonbenefit rewards. However, they mostly focus on providing competitive benefits and directing the efforts of creativity and design concern to the compensation and other rewards side of the total rewards equation. Cutting benefit costs is a way to try to get additional money to fund attempts to create organizations that brand themselves to attract the type of employee they believe will add most value to the enterprise.

From 'Best Place to Work' to 'Best *High-Performance* Place to Work'

Total rewards professionals must take hold of "best place to work" designations to get a seat at the business strategy table. Conflicting messages often come from initiatives about reducing benefits costs dramatically and at the same time focusing on actions to become a best place to work.

Publications such as *Working Mother* and *Fortune* annually sponsor the opportunity for companies to become designated best places to work. As an offshoot, many HR associations have become strong advocates of proactively enhancing the workplace to make work more acceptable and engaging. They have suggested that organizations that become more family friendly or facilitate working from home are better places to work than organizations that do not provide such advantages.

However, there is only anecdotal information about the possible influence that becoming a best place to work has in recruiting and keeping *high* performers and little about how such actions might facilitate improved employee performance.

Is there evidence to suggest that reducing employee benefits and adding workplace improvements on the nonbenefit side of the ledger is adding value to organizational performance? Independent research is needed.

Organizations are deeply involved in passing health-care costs on to employees and reducing retirement benefits while at the same time focusing on work-life benefits such as the opportunity for sabbaticals or the chance to share jobs and spend portions of their work time working at home rather than coming to the office. What messages are these organizations sending to their workforce?

Does it make sense for an organization to become a best place to work with the notion that they distinguished themselves for some significant move favoring creating a family-friendly workplace while at the same time health-care benefits and retirement benefits are significantly reduced? Does the breadwinner go home and say, "I just got a sabbatical leave after 10 years of service, and by the way, we have less medical coverage."

The most startling missing element from best places to work initiatives is that they are silent on issues such as creating a workplace where skill and competency growth is meaningfully rewarded. Probably most important is a lack of recognition for organizations that are successful in really and meaningfully creating a workplace where performance excellence is transparently and consistently rewarded and encouraged.

It would be useful to see an organization become a best place to work because it has a working total rewards program driven by clear ways to reward the acquisition and application of key skills and competencies to the performance equation. Although there is clear evidence that organizations that actually pay for goal achievement are much more likely to engage employees to help them succeed and thereby really be more likely to meet goals, no evidence suggests being a best place to work at the expense of benefits or paying for performance helps organizations become high-performance workplaces.

What comes first—the performance or the programs? Indeed, the usual route to trying to become a preferred workplace is to first be a successful enterprise and then or concurrently implement what leadership believes is an employee-positive work environment. Few poor-performing organizations report that they obtained top performance from employees or attracted people of great value by a turnaround strategy driven by sabbatical leaves for employees.

Total rewards professionals need to explore the overall impact and direction in which the business is moving to prove they are viable business partners. This is not a case against becoming a best place to work; rather, it is a suggestion that companies consider the direction that this goal produces and perhaps ask some key and defining questions. The objective should be to become a "best *high-performance* place to work."

New Directions and Priorities

Why should total rewards professionals become increasingly concerned about the above issues? Total rewards professionals play the most important role in HR relative to facilitating an organization's journey to become a high-performance enterprise through compensation, benefits and other rewards. Yet the career path to the most responsible HR slot in most organizations does not often enough come through the compensation or benefits professional paths.

Instead, professionals from employee relations, training, development, recruitment or labor relations are more likely to get the HR function's seat at the senior strategy table than are those professionals with careers in compensation and benefits. This is a flawed approach. Total rewards professionals with a total rewards approach should be on a fast track to a strategic role and the preferred source of HR leaders.

Among the largest costs most organizations face are associated with the workforce—compensation and benefits costs are one of the largest expenses for nearly every organization. And total rewards professional roles are the most influential HR roles in managing these costs effectively. The answer to getting a contributing strategy seat is to bring total rewards together into an integrated strategic move to help facilitate creating a high-performance workplace. The HR professions dedicated to training, development, labor relations and recruitment are putting together a powerful business case for professionals in these arenas to become HR leaders. The time is now for the compensation and benefits professions in the form of total rewards professionals to do this as well.

High-Performance Organizations

What organizations should total rewards professionals benchmark as models to emulate? It is clear that Wal-Mart is a dominant company that has changed the retail business forever. Is it a high-performance organization? It has built a successful organization with a loyal and hard-working workforce with compensation and benefits that many conclude are far below competitive practice in any area in which they choose to operate.

How about Ford and General Motors? Clearly they have a tradition of liberal and expensive compensation and benefits, and many believe they also may have created an "encrusted" culture of entitlement throughout their workforce. They do not fit a definition of a high-performance workplace.

Wal-Mart and GM and Ford are at different ends of the compensation and benefits spectrum. Wal-Mart is growing, doing well, and expanding market share. GM and Ford seem to be proving that the creation of a workplace based on tenure and entitlement and the eventual loss of market dominance may be positively related. And what of the airlines and how they fit in defining a high-performance workplace? Is Southwest the model to be followed by Northwest, United and Delta?

Total rewards professionals work in all these organizations and try to align a total rewards strategy with a workable business model for success. Does this mean however that the more you reduce compensation and benefits, the better your company will perform?

From the workforce perspective, a high-performance organization is one where the deal that exists between the organization and its people builds an accurate set of expectations on the part of the organization's leaders and its employees accountable for results. Whatever you think of Wal-Mart's total rewards strategy, it has been consistent since the creation of the company. It did not offer liberal compensation and benefits and then change this strategy midcareer for its workforce. On the other hand, the auto companies and airlines tried to change the deal they made with their workforces midcareer. And this is a critical lesson about basing pay on tenure and entitlement.

Auto and airline companies have not been able to reinvent themselves to produce products and services that their customers would buy at a price that covered the cost of doing business. They cannot pass on high guaranteed compensation and benefits costs to customers without corresponding product and service performance improvements. So their total rewards strategies possibly accelerated the demise of their industry leadership position. What role, if any, did total rewards professionals play in these debacles?

The Quest for Talent

Historically, organizations spend more money when the market for skills and competencies is tight. Then, as soon as business slows they reduce the workforce—often without closely studying its impact on the organization's future. Someone needs to question these practices and encourage company leadership to be more selective in providing criteria to define who goes and who stays based on what makes sense to the organization's future.

While total rewards professionals make recommendations and provide advice to CEOs who ultimately make decisions about how total rewards are to be managed, total rewards professionals should promote the following priorities:

- **Communications and education:** Institute a "no surprises" training and communication program for new hires when they enter the organization and periodically throughout their career. Communicate policy on changing total rewards and make sure employees understand that total rewards strategies and tactics may change as business and other conditions change. Address feelings of entitlement and compensation and benefits based only on tenure early and constantly. Make it clear that the organization emphasizes a win-win partnership that requires employees to add value throughout their careers to remain with the organization.

- **Pay for performance:** Implement metrics that set performance standards and make sure everyone understands how they influence key yardsticks of organizational success. It is essential for total rewards professionals to take the lead on paying for and rewarding performance. Many organizations do not really pay for performance and give the concept only lip service. Making it clear that performance counts gives the organization the chance to be attractive to people who are willing to have their performance evaluated and to managers who are willing to evaluate the performance of others.

- **Total rewards career path:** No more compensation and benefits professionals should be trained separately. It is a total rewards profession, and the career path must include experience in compensation and benefits. It must involve education about total compensation and how compensation and benefits relate to the overall programs and performance of the organization. Professional development must cover the link between compensation and benefits from a rewards perspective and from the standpoint of effective total rewards cost management. It must also address the integration and balance of the total rewards package, including all elements of total rewards.

- **Reward superkeepers first:** Not everyone in an organization is equally critical to its success. Providing compensation and benefits in equal shares to all makes little sense. Total rewards are an economic issue, and priority needs to go to the people with the critical skills that can generate business results. Most organizations make little difference between the rewards they grant to the best performers and those that most employees receive. Total rewards professionals can make the difference. If the organization wants its share of the top 20 percent of the performers, it is essential to make it evident that becoming a high performer is rewarded and recognized.

Organizations are under siege to produce total rewards strategies that are designed to focus on the best people—not on everyone. The HR function, led by total rewards professionals, needs to develop solutions that permit the recognition of differences in value added based on demonstrated skills, competencies, performance and business results. Then the seat at the strategy table will be in focus.

Conclusions

It is time for compensation and benefits professionals to become total rewards professionals and to receive more attention and recognition. They are in the right place, at the right time, with the tools and business case to become even more essential than ever before to their organization's performance. Total rewards, including compensation and benefits, brand the organization and communicate to employees what it is like to work there.

Total rewards professionals must increase their value to avoid having their core professions become increasingly outsourced. This means internal total rewards professionals must serve as important in-house consultants, advisors, communicators, program designers and facilitators whom organizations need for managing their largest expense—compensation and benefits.

Compensation and benefits professionals must become total rewards professionals. Organizations are in crisis, struggling to gain maximum mileage and value from total rewards and expenditures on compensation and benefits. Talent is getting increasingly scarce, and CEOs are saying they want more return from the money and time invested on total rewards. They are critical of HR for spending too much time on the "soft" parts of the people challenge. Total rewards are important change agents that quickly command the attention of the workforce. They can enlist the support of the workforce in helping the organization grow and be successful.

Notes
1 "B" players may not result in lower performance, but will not likely result in higher performance.

First published in *Compensation & Benefits Review*, May/June 2006, 38 (3), 18-23. Reprinted by permission of SAGE Publications Inc.

Articles by Patricia K. Zingheim and Jay R. Schuster

Zingheim, P.K., J.R. Schuster and D.A. Thomsen. 2005. "Executive Compensation: Rewarding Excellence and Ensuring Governance." *Nonprofit World*, September/October: 14-17.

Thomsen, D.J. and J.R. Schuster. 2005. "The 'Not-for-Profit' Hotseat." *Human Resource Executive*, Oct. 2: 56-58.

Zingheim, P.K., J.R. Schuster and D.A. Thomsen. 2005. "Is Your Nonprofit Board Prepared for the Executive Compensation Crisis?" *Directors Monthly*, July: 18-19.

Zingheim, P.K., J.R. Schuster and D.A. Thomsen. 2005. "The Executive Compensation Crisis in Tax-Exempt Organizations." *PIHRAScope*, March/April: 8-11.

Zingheim, P.K., J.R. Schuster and D.A. Thomsen. 2005. "Executive Compensation: Rewarding Excellence and Ensuring Governance." *MWorld*, Spring: 22-24.

Zingheim, P.K. and J.R. Schuster. 2005. "The Next Decade for Pay and Rewards." *Compensation & Benefits Review*, January/February: 26-32.

Zingheim, P.K. 2004. "Compensating Superkeepers: Talent Your Company Needs to Thrive." In L.A. Berger and D.R. Berger (eds.), *The Talent Management Handbook: Creating Organizational Excellence by Identifying, Developing, & Promoting Your Best People*. New York: McGraw-Hill.

Schuster, J.R. and P.K. Zingheim. 2004. "Compensating Superkeepers." In *Thoughts from the Top: A Collection of Interviews with Business Gurus*. Aurora, ON, Canada: HR.com Publishing.

Zingheim, P.K. and J.R. Schuster. 2004. "How to Develop a Workable Incentive Plan: HR's Major 'ROI' Reward Opportunity." *PIHRAScope*, October/November: 8-9 and 30-33.

Schuster, J.R. and P.K. Zingheim. 2004. "Total Rewards: People Want More Than Money." *Executive Excellence*, January: 5.

Zingheim, P.K. and J.R. Schuster. 2003. "Winning Your Organisation's Battle for Superkeepers." *New Zealand Security*, December: 36-44.

Zingheim, P.K. and J.R. Schuster. 2003. "Bring Practical Total Rewards to Your Organization." *PIHRAScope*, November: 8-9 and 20-21.

Zingheim, P.K. and J.R. Schuster. 2003. "Expert Advice: How Can You Ensure '04 Is More Profitable?" *IOMA's Pay for Performance Report*, November: 2-5.

Gentilo, E., K. Hudson, J.R. Schuster and P.K. Zingheim. 2003. "Customer-First Rewards: New Performance Directions for Public Power." *APPA's People to People*, Summer: 1 and 6-7.

Zingheim, P.K. and J.R. Schuster. 2003. "Getting Back to Basics." *workspan*, May: 54-58.

Zingheim, P.K. and J.R. Schuster. 2002. "In a Downturn, Do You Cut Pay, Slash the Workforce, or Protect Precious Talent?" *Strategy & Leadership*. January/February: 23-26.

Zingheim, P.K. and J.R. Schuster. 2002. "Aligning Total Rewards for Global Economic Recovery." *workspan*, May: 20-26.

Zingheim, P.K. and J.R. Schuster. 2002. "Executive Incentives." *Executive Excellence*, March: 5.

Zingheim, P.K. and J.R. Schuster. 2002. "Pay It Forward." *People Management*, Feb. 7: 32-34.

Zingheim, P.K. and J.R. Schuster. 2002. "Cut Pay or Cut Back?" *Executive Excellence*, January: 16-17.

Zingheim, P.K. and J.R. Schuster. 2001. "Managing in Tough Economic Times." *Chartered Financial Analyst*, December: 34-36.

Zingheim, P.K. and J.R. Schuster. 2001. "Getting Ahead in the Reward Game." *Strategy & Leadership*, November/December: 34-36.

Zingheim, P.K. and J.R. Schuster. 2001. "How You Pay Is What You Get." *Across the Board*, September/October: 41-44.

Zingheim, P.K. and J.R. Schuster. 2001. "Manufacturing Slump! What about Pay for a Manufacturing Workforce." *The Ohio Manufacturer*, September: 1 and 4-5.

Zingheim, P.K. and J.R. Schuster. 2001. "Manufacturing Slump! What about Pay for a Manufacturing Workforce." *Manufacturer of Michigan*, September: 1 and 7.

Zingheim, P.K. and J.R. Schuster. 2001. "Manufacturing Slump! What about Pay for a Manufacturing Workforce." *The Kentucky Manufacturer*, September: 8 and 17.

Zingheim, P.K. and J.R. Schuster. 2001. "Manufacturing Slump! What about Pay for a Manufacturing Workforce." *The Indiana Manufacturer*, September: 1 and 4.

Zingheim, P.K. and J.R. Schuster. 2001. "Paying Smart." *Executive Excellence*, July: 11.

Zingheim, P.K. and J.R. Schuster. 2001. "Winning the Talent Game: Total Rewards and the Better Workforce Deal!" *Compensation & Benefits Management*, Summer: 33-39.

Zingheim, P.K. and J.R. Schuster. 2001. "Designing Pay and Rewards to Make M&A's Work." *Compensation & Benefits Review*, May/June: 32-36.

Zingheim, P.K. and J.R. Schuster. 2001. "Using the Pay System as a Rallying Point for Merged Workforces." *Mergers & Acquisitions*, May: 37-44.

Zingheim, P.K. and J.R. Schuster. 2001. "Retaining Top Talent." *Executive Excellence*, March: 20.

Zingheim, P.K. and J.R. Schuster. 2001. "Fair Pay." *US Industry Today*, March: 7.

Zingheim, P.K. and J.R. Schuster. 2001. "Powering Up Rewards for the Fast-Moving Economy." *The Financial Manager*, February/March: 27-29.

Zingheim, P.K. and J.R. Schuster. 2001. "Pay Readiness and Other Devices: An Evaluation of the Sales IQ of Life Insurance Companies." *Insurance Advocate*, February: 40-44.

Zingheim, P.K. and J.R. Schuster. 2001. "Long-Term Variable Pay: An Accelerator Pedal for Total Rewards." *Compensation & Benefits Management*, Winter: 36-48.

Zingheim, P.K. "Rewarding Scarce Talent." 2000. In L.A. Berger and D.R. Berger (eds.), *The Compensation Handbook*. New York: McGraw-Hill.

Zingheim, P.K. and J.R. Schuster. 2000. "High Performance Rewards." *Oil & Gas Journal*, Dec. 11: 26-30.

Zingheim, P.K. and J.R. Schuster. 2000. "Tips to Help Your Company Keep the Best Employees." *High Volume Printing*, December: 20-24.

Zingheim, P.K. and J.R. Schuster. 2000. "Performance Pays." *Pharmaceutical Executive*, December: 68-73.

Zingheim, P.K. and J.R. Schuster. 2000. "Total Rewards for New and Old Economy Companies." *Compensation & Benefits Review*, November/December: 20-23.

Zingheim, P.K. and J.R. Schuster. 2000. "Pay People Right! Keeping Top Technical Talent." *IT Professional*, November/December: 45-48.

Zingheim, P.K. and J.R. Schuster. 2000. "Pay Innovators Right!" *Innovative Leader*, October: 1-3, 8.

Zingheim, P.K. 2000. "Expert Advice on Pay Design." *workspan*, September: 58. (Book review of *Aligning Pay and Results*, by Howard Risher).

Zingheim, P.K. and J.R. Schuster. 2000. "Doing Your Executive Comp Deal?" *Executive Talent*, Fall: 68-73.

Zingheim, P.K. and J.R. Schuster. 2000. "Total Rewards: Pushing the Pedal to the Metal." *Journal of Business Strategy*, July/August: 15-17.

Zingheim, P.K. and J.R. Schuster. 2000. "'E-Pay' Changes Compensation—Forever." *Harvard Management Update*, May: 10.

Schuster, J.R. 2000. "Book Delivers Pay Strategies for New Economy." *ACA News*, May: 50. (Book review of *Rewarding Excellence*, by Edward E. Lawler III).

Zingheim, P.K. and J.R. Schuster. 2000. "Total Rewards." *Human Resource Executive*, April: A20-A22.

Zingheim, P.K. and J.R. Schuster. 2000. "Before It's Too Late: When to Change Your Pay Package." *Across the Board*, March: 23-27.

Zingheim, P.K. and J.R. Schuster. 1999. "Rewards for Scarce Information Technology Talent." *ACA Journal*, Fourth Quarter: 48-57.

Zingheim, P.K. and J.R. Schuster. 1999. "Dealing with Scarce Talent: Lessons from the Leading Edge." *Compensation & Benefits Review*, March/April: 36-44.

Zingheim, P.K. and J.R. Schuster. 1999. "Variable Pay: Right for Your Healthcare Organization Now?" *HHRMAC News*, March: 23-25.

Zingheim, P.K. and J.R. Schuster. 1997. "How to Pay Members of Small, High-Performance Teams." In *Team Pay Case Studies: What's Working in Companies Today*, a Special Report from *Compensation & Benefits Review*.

Zingheim, P.K. and J.R. Schuster. 1997. "Compensation Strategy: 'New Pay' Deployed to Advance Organizational Goals at Three California Hospitals." *Strategies for Healthcare Excellence*, August: 9-12.

Schuster, J.R. and P.K. Zingheim. 1997. "Reinventing Federal Pay: How One Agency Is Succeeding." *ACA News*, June: 12-15.

Zingheim, P.K. and J.R. Schuster. 1997. "Best Practices for Small-Team Pay." *ACA Journal*, Spring: 40-49.

Zingheim, P.K., G.E. Ledford Jr. and J.R. Schuster. 1996. "Competencies and Competency Models: Does One Size Fit All?" *ACA Journal*, Spring: 56-65.

Zingheim, P.K. and J.R. Schuster. 1995. "First Findings: The Team Pay Research Study." *Compensation & Benefits Review*, November-December: 6-14.

Zingheim, P.K. and J.R. Schuster. 1995. "Exploring Three Pay Transition Tools: Readiness Assessment, Benchmarking, and Piloting." *Compensation & Benefits Review*, July-August: 40-45.

Zingheim, P.K. and J.R. Schuster. 1995. "Introduction: How Are the New Pay Tools Being Deployed?" *Compensation & Benefits Review*, July-August: 10-13.

Zingheim, P.K. and J.R. Schuster. 1995. "Moving One Notch North: Executing the Transition to New Pay." *Compensation & Benefits Review*, July-August: 33-39.

Zingheim, P.K. and J.R. Schuster. 1995. "Supporting Teams with Multi-Rater Performance Reviews." *Compensation & Benefits Management*, Summer: 41-45.

Zingheim, P.K. 1995. "Making Rewards Work: Communicating Strategic Alignment through Rewards." *ACA Journal*, Summer: 27-30.

Zingheim, P.K. and J.R. Schuster. 1995. "Time for a Serious Look at New Pay in Canada." *Compensation News*, May: 2-13.

Zingheim, P.K. 1995. "Time for a New Look at New Pay." *ACA News*, January: 2 and 10.

Zingheim, P.K. and J.R. Schuster. 1994. "Lessons from Asia in Paying Teams and Rewarding Enterprise." *Journal of International Compensation & Benefits*, July/August: 1-4.

Zingheim, P.K. 1994. "How to Make Performance Pay a Reality." *Healthcare Human Resources*, March: 9-10.

Schuster, J.R. and P.K. Zingheim. 1993. "Building Pay Environments to Facilitate High-Performance Teams." *ACA Journal*, Spring/Summer: 40-51.

Schuster, J.R. and P.K. Zingheim. 1993. "'New Pay' Strategies That Work." *Journal of Compensation and Benefits*, May/June: 5-9.

Schuster, J.R. and P.K. Zingheim. 1993. "The New Variable Pay: Key Design Issues." *Compensation & Benefits Review*, March/April: 27-34.

Schuster, J.R. and P.K. Zingheim. 1993. "New Pay in Major U.S. Companies." *HR Horizons*, Spring: 5-12.

Zingheim, P.K. and J.R. Schuster. 1992. "Linking Quality and Pay." *HR Magazine*, December: 55-59.

Kitsuse, A. 1992. "Down with Merit-Pay Increases: An Interview with J.R. Schuster and P.K. Zingheim." *Conference Board*, November: 23-27.

Schuster, J.R., P.K. Zingheim and M.G. Dertien. 1990. "The Case for Computer-Assisted Market-Based Job Evaluation." *Compensation and Benefits Review*, May/June: 44-54.

Schuster, J.R. and P.K. Zingheim. 1990. "Managing Human Resources in a Merger." *Compensation & Benefits Management*, Spring: 230-233.

Schuster, J.R. and P.K. Zingheim. 1989. "New Compensation Planning Needed for Labor-Intensive Organizations." *Journal of Compensation and Benefits*, November/December: 157-161.

Schuster, J.R. and P.K. Zingheim. 1989. "How Productivity-Based Pay Works in Retail Banking." *The Bankers Magazine*, May/June: 62-66.

Schuster, J.R. and P.K. Zingheim. 1989. "Improving Productivity through Gainsharing: Can the Means Be Justified in the End?" *Compensation & Benefits Management*, Spring: 207-210.

Schuster, J.R. and P.K. Zingheim. 1988. "Incentive Plans that Work." *ABA Banking Journal*, September: 62-64.

Schuster, J.R. and P.K. Zingheim. 1987. "Merit Pay: Is It Hopeless in the Public Sector?" *Personnel Administrator*, October. 83-84.

Schuster, J.R. and P.K. Zingheim. 1986. "Incentives for Performance: How Much More Positive Proof Do We Need?" *Compensation & Benefits Management*, Autumn: 405-407.

Schuster, J.R. and P.K. Zingheim. 1986. "Tying Compensation to Top Performance Can Boost Profits." *Journal of Compensation and Benefits*, September/October: 69-73.

Schuster, J.R. and P.K. Zingheim. 1986. "Sales Compensation Strategies at the Most Successful Companies." *Personnel Journal*, June: 112-116.

Schuster, J.R. and P.K. Zingheim. 1986. "Designing Incentives for Top Financial Performance." *Compensation and Benefits Review*, May/June: 39-48.

Schuster, J.R. 1985. "How to Control Job Evaluation Inflation." *Personnel Administrator*, June: 167-173.

Schuster, J.R. 1985. "Compensation Plan Design: the Power behind the Best High-Tech Companies." *Management Review*, May: 21-25.

Schuster, J.R. 1985. "Successful Hospitals Pay for Performance." *Hospitals*, March: 86-87.

Schuster, J.R. 1973. "The Cafeteria Benefits Line." *Pension and Welfare News*, October: 57-59.

Schuster, J.R. 1973. "The Relationship between Perceptions Concerning Magnitudes of Pay and the Perceived Utility of Pay: Public and Private Organizations Compared." *Organization Behavior and Human Performance*, February: 110-119.

Schuster, J.R. 1972. "Flexible Compensation." *Personnel Administration and Public Personnel Review*, November/December: 12-16.

Schuster, J.R., B. Clark and M. Rogers. 1971. "Testing Portions of the Porter and Lawler Model Regarding the Motivational Role of Pay." *Journal of Applied Psychology*. 187-195.

Schuster, J.R. 1971. "Toward a Direct-Contribution Reinforcement Pay System." *Management of Personnel Quarterly*, Spring: 2-5.

Schuster, J.R., L.D. Hart, and B. Clark. 1971. "EPIC: New Cafeteria Compensation Plan." *Datamation*, February: 28-30.

Schuster, J.R. 1969. "A Spectrum of Pay for Performance: How to Motivate Employees." *Management of Personnel Quarterly*, Fall: 35-38.

Schuster, J.R. 1969. "Another Look at Compensation Preferences." *Industrial Management Review*, Sloan School of Management, 1-18.

Index

Benefits, 3, 42, 151; liberal, 28, 29, 151; predicting the future of total pay, 154, 155; total compensation perspective in executive compensation, 114; and total rewards professionals, 157-165

Best companies, 29, 30; characteristics of, 28

Best *High-Performance* Place to Work: from Best Place to Work to, 160-162

Best people, 6, 26, 44, 151, 165; keeping, 89. *See also* Superkeepers

Best Place to Work 18, 19, 154; to Best *High-Performance* Place to Work, 160-162; period and scarce talent and total pay design: realities come home to roost, 151; and workplace brand 28, 29

Best place workforce, 32

Best practice, 60, 115, 144, 145; incentives for contact centers and distribution centers: driving customer satisfaction, 57-65; in performance management priorities, 35-38; setting stretch performance expectations, 52

Best-of-the-best talent, 17

Better workforce deal: and total rewards and total pay design, realities come home to roost, 151-152

BMW, 27

Board, 36, 115; and executive compensation within nonprofits, 119-129; HR committee, 116

Board of directors: protecting tax-exempt boards and organizations, 124-126

Board of Governors, USPS, 134

Board members: consequences of intermediate sanctions to within nonprofits, 121-123

Brand, 5, 6, 19, 86, 160, 165; creating powerful customized workplace rewards, 27-32. *See also* Workplace Brands

Branding, 151

Broadbanding, 77

Burning platform, 24, 46

Business case, 7, 8, 10, 12, 14, 17, 26, 58, 59, 89, 105, 113, 120, 123, 134, 150, 162, 165; example incentives not-for-profit medical group, 51; for incentive plan, 46; pay for performance works: U.S. Postal Service presents a powerful, 12-13, 131-140; USPS shows success, 140

Business goal plan: choose the right incentive design, 49

Business goals, 4, 28, 63, 70, 72, 90, 95; and contact center metrics, 60; six principles of total rewards, 42

Business leaders, 2, 10, 17

Business metrics, 31, 151; deploy clear, business performance culture branding, 30

Business performance, 52, 91; accelerating with incentives, 7-8, 39-65; culture branding, 30-31

Business plan, 11, 21, 53, 105, 106, 107, 127; and sales incentive goals, 109, 110; setting stretch performance expectations, 52

Business strategy, 160; changing incentive goals in mid-performance period, 53; a new look at pay, 41; one company's experience with performance management, 34; and superkeepers, 18, 20, 25; and workplace branding, 31

Business value, 6, 17, 72, 142, 154; and paying for skill and the Internet, 10, 95-101

C

Call time, 61

Call volume, 51, 61

Capabilities, 5, 11, 17, 30, 64, 75, 82, 143; and competencies, 85, 87, 89; sales pay tune up, 106; and sales rewards, 107, 108, 111; and skills, 91, 93, 94

Capitalizing on Human Assets, 45

Career, 150

Customer partnerships, 8; and incentive principles in contact center and distribution centers, 58

Customer satisfaction, 35, 41, 42, 57, 61, 91, 140; driving with best practice incentives for contact centers and distribution centers, 8, 57-65; example not-for-profit organization goals and business case, 51; example storewide incentive measures, 48-49; performance measures and categories, 47

Customer service, 12, 47, 48, 51, 64, 131, 136; and contact centers and distribution centers, 57, 59

Customer service organization, telephone: and incentives, 50-51

Customer service representatives, 7, 8, 57, 91. *See also* CSRs

Customers, target, 11; sales pay tune-up, 106, 107; update and sales rewards, 110-111

Customization 7, 65, 156; allow for within the organization, 21; incentive design, 50; reward, 2, 3

Customize 5, 49; to your organization: ten performance management priorities, 33, 35-36

Customized, 3, 85; workplace rewards brand, creating a powerful, 6, 27-32

Cycle time, 61

D

Databases: and market data, 80-81

Deal: employment, 30, 152. *See also* New workforce deal; Better workforce deal

Define performance: ten performance management priorities, 33, 35

Delta Airlines, 163

Differences, 70; meaningful reward, 134, 135-137

Disney, 27

Distribution centers, 7, 8, 57-65

Distribution centers, best practice incentives for: 8, 57-65; award frequency, 62; award size, 63; communication, 63, conclusion, 65; goal setting, 62; incentive design, 59-64; incentive principles, 58-59; integration with other reward components, 63-64, metrics, 60-62; supervisors, 64; unit of measurement, 59-60

Drive business success, 1, 7

Dropped calls as percent of total calls, 61

E

Economic recovery: and total pay design: realities come home to roost, 152

Economy, fast-moving: powering up incentives for, 7, 41-44

Educate, 2, 44, 54, 88, 115

Educated, three critical steps to protect executive compensation from IRS challenge, 128

Education, 28, 37, 53, 88, 99, 154, 164

Educational, 13, 88, 111

Elevator speech, 92

Emphasize results: business performance culture branding, 30

Employee performance, 33, 38, 69, 70, 72, 95, 154, 160

Employee success, 1

Employer of preference, 19, 29

Employers of choice, 28

Encourage to leave: selective talent strategies, 20

Engage, 44

Engage employees, 161; in performance management process: ten performance management priorities, 33, 37

Engage managers: ten performance management priorities, 33, 35

Engage people, 1, 72

Engage workforce, 6, 14, 34, 63, 64

Engaged, 3, 157

Engagement, 2, 154; communication of incentive design in contact centers and distribution centers, 63

Enron, 119

Entitlement, 3, 12, 18, 36, 46, 54, 69, 70, 114, 115, 117, 149, 164; and high-performance organizations, 163

Entitlement period: and total pay design: realities come home to roost, 149-150

Equity, 12, 20, 42, 43, 153, 154; internal, 3, 55, 59, 76, 77, 149, 150

Equity incentives: predicting the future of total pay, 154

ERI's *Compensation Comparables Assessor and Tax-Exempt Survey*, 121

ERI's *Executive Compensation Assessor*, 121

E-survey sources: the technology factor in job valuing, 81-82

EVA Variable Pay Program (USPS), 135, 139

Executive compensation: doing the heavy lifting, 11-12, 113-117; future is now, 117; HR leader's advising role, 116; performance shares lead the way, 115-116; total compensation perspective, 114-115

Executive Compensation Assessor, 121

Executive compensation within nonprofits: conclusions and suggestions, 128-129; consequences of intermediate sanctions to board members, 121-123; example of intermediate sanctions, 126-127; example of paying for performance with reasonable compensation at a hospital, 127-128; intermediate sanctions, 120-121; involvement of states in reasonable compensation, 123; protecting tax-exempt boards and organizations, 124-

126; reasons for paying for performance, 123-124; rewarding excellence and ensuring governance, 12, 119-129; three critical steps to protect from IRS challenge, 128

Executive performance, 12, 120, 123, 124, 125, 128

Executive rewards, 12, 117, 120, 125

Executive talent, attract and retain: reasons for paying for performance in nonprofits, 124

Executives: communicated and championed competency-based pay solutions, 88

Extension of the business, 13; and incentive principles in contact center and distribution centers, 58

External market, 9, 76, 79, 81, 87, 97, 149; and elements of job value, 78

External marketplace, 20, 77, 79, 87, 88

F

Fair Labor Standards Act (FLSA), 63

Fairness, 2, 3, 20, 72

Federal Times, 140

Feedback, 4, 7, 20, 34, 37, 58, 59, 61, 62, 63, 64, 72, 95, 139, 143; ten performance management priorities, 33, 36-37

Feedback and dialogue, 7; ten performance management priorities, 33, 36-37

Few metrics, 8; and incentive principles in contact center and distribution centers, 58

Financial compensation, 133, 140

Ford, 162, 163

Form 990, 121

Form 990PF, 121

Forms and formats: selecting pay and rewards computer and Web-based products, 144

Fortune, 28, 29, 151, 160

Free agent (employee), 152, 156

Functional area, 38, 82; compensable elements, 79-80

Future, the, 13, 14, 156, 163; can base pay reward performance, 74; and benefits, 155; career directions for total rewards professionals, 157; is now in executive compensation, 117; predicting the, 153-156; superkeepers, 26; and total pay design: realities come home to roost, 152-153; workplace total pay, 154

Future-focused, 43, 47, 49

G

Gainsharing plan, choose the right incentive design, 49

General Electric, 27, 42

General Mills, 27, 43

General Motors (GM), 162, 163

Global, 95, 150, 151, 155; recession 149; 2000-2002 recession and Sept. 11 period: and total pay design: realities come home to roost, 152

Goal setting, 7, 19, 34, 36, 51, 72, 106, 124, 128, 155; belief system concerning performance management and management of people, 4; for incentive design in contact centers and distribution centers, 62; setting stretch performance expectations, 52

Goals: key, 7, 43, 81, 134, 144; and measures, put the right amount of stretch in, 45, 51; set stretch, 43. *See also* Incentive goals; Performance goals

Governance, 11, 116; ensuring, and rewarding excellence in executive compensation within nonprofits, 12, 119-129; protecting tax exempt boards and organizations, 124

Governance, corporate, 119, 123; three critical steps to protect executive compensation from IRS challenge, 128, 129

H

Hay, Ned, 141

Hay plan, 76, 81. *See also* Point factor

HealthPartners, 123, 125

High performance: belief system concerning performance management and management of people, 4; belief system concerning the total pay component of total rewards, 3; belief system concerning total rewards other than total pay, 5; creating, 3-4; nonprofit, 121; organizations, 162-163

High-Performance Pay: Fast Forward to Business Success, 1, 4, 14; basis for, 2

High-performing: people, 6, 89, 117. *See also* Superkeepers; Top 20 percent

High-technology, 23, 36, 41. *See also* Technology

High-technology company: and proof of superkeeper talent strategy, 23.

Hospital: example of paying for performance with reasonable compensation in nonprofit, 127-128

Hot change, 54, 87, 142

HR, 113, 162, at the center of, 159; leaders' advising role, 116

HR champions, 159

I

IBM, 43, 153

Incentive design: choose the right, 49-51; for contact centers and distribution centers, 59-64; seven principles of, 45. *See also* Incentive design, effective

Incentive design, effective: choose the right performance measures, 46-49; communicate and champion, 54-55, don't give up, 55; evaluate outcomes and change as needed, 53-54; know why incentives will help, 46; measure performance where is counts the most, 51-53;

IRS, 114; and executive compensation within nonprofits, 120-129; Exempt Organizations Division, 120-121; Exempt Organizations Electronics Initiative Office, 120-121; technical advice memoranda (TAM) on intermediate sanctions, 126

J

Job descriptions, 76, 95

Job evaluation, 9, 81, 97; in entitlement period, 149

Job matching, 77

Job valuation: reasons for, 75-76

Job valuing, 9, 150; and compensable elements, 80; and market data, 80-81; and more verification of market ranking process, 77; move to market pricing, 76-77; new solutions, 78-79; and the people-based solution, 83; and the point factor plan, 141-142; reasons for job valuation, 75-76; status of today, 77-78; and the technology factor, 81-82

Justify the application: pre-approving skill-based pay, 93

K

Knowledge, 9, 64, 78, 85, 142, 149; and expertise: executive compensation within nonprofits, 122, 126, 127

L

Labor market, 10, 21, 42, 72; competency pay connected to, 87-88; example of paying for performance with reasonable compensation at a hospital (nonprofit), 127-128

Labor market, competitive, 23, 72; action step to help paying for performance, 73

Lack of critique capability: selecting pay and rewards computer and Web-based products, 144

Lack of uniqueness: selecting pay and rewards computer and Web-based products, 144

Language skills, compensable elements, 80

Lawler, Ed, 152

Leaders, 1, 17

Leaders, HR, 11, 38, 57, 113, 115, 117, 162; advising role in executive compensation, 116

Leadership, 87, 158; champions of pay for performance at U.S. Postal Service, 134

Leadership accountability, compensable elements, 80

Learning and experience: compensable elements, 80

Less than high performance: belief system concerning performance management and management of people, 4; belief system concerning the total pay component of total rewards, 3; belief system concerning total rewards other than total pay, 5

Line of sight, 4, 50, 109, 154; and communication, 63; measure performance where it counts most, 51-53; six principles of total rewards, 42, 43; USPS performance metric weighting for, 135; weightings of performance metrics, 137; what incentives can do, 47

Linking Quality and Pay, 57

Long-term compensation, 11, 113, 114, 115

Long-term variable pay, 22, 25

M

Management of costs: selecting pay and rewards computer and Web-based products, 143. *See also* Cost management

Managers, 34, 35, 36, 37, 38; action step to help paying for performance, 72

Managers, group of: action step to help paying for performance, 72

S

Salary increase budget, 9, 73, 155

Sales compensation, 11, 105-112; ensure competitive total cash, 107-108; ensure a proper base-incentive mix, 108; paying selling professionals, 105-107; reinforce critical selling behaviors, 111-112; set realistic performance goals, 109-110; suggestions and opportunities, 112; time for a high-performance sales pay tune up, 106; tuning up, 107; update incentive measures, 109; update target customers, 110-111

Sales goals, 106, 108, 109, 110

Sales incentive plans, 50, 105; set realistic performance goals, 109-110

Sales incentives, 106, 109, 110, 111

Sales professionals, 11, 70; and sales rewards, 105, 106, 107, 108, 109, 110, 111

Sales rewards solutions, 11, 105-112. *See also* Sales compensation

Sales volume, 48, 106, 108, 110; update sales rewards incentive measures, 109

Sarbanes-Oxley Act, 95

Scarce talent, 149, 154, 159; and best places to work period and total pay design: realities come home to roost, 151; and superkeepers, 17

Schuster-Zingheim and Associates, 57

Securities and Exchange Commission (SEC), 113; disclosure rules, 113, 114

Selection, 18, 21, 82, 96, 142; recruitment and placement and: Internet and paying for skills, 99

Sept. 11 period and 2000-2002 global recession: and total pay design: realities come home to roost, 152

SERP, 113, 114

Skill and competency, 4, 75; business performance culture branding, 30-31; paying for on the Web, 82. *See also* Skills and competencies

Skill growth, 91

Skill pay, 10, 100; Internet tools for, 98-99, programming: Internet and paying for skills, 98. *See also* Skill-based pay

Skill performance management: Internet and paying for skills, 98-99

Skill program, in contact centers, 64

Skill training and development, 100; Internet and paying for skills, 99

Skill-based pay, 153; assessing the value of, 10, 91-94; cranking up the engine, 92-94; kick start, 92; program should include, 92; requires clarity in, 91; where can add most value, 94. *See also* Skill pay

Skill-profiling capability: Internet and paying for skills, 98

Skills and competencies, critical, 3, 4, 6, 72, 77, 152; and base pay adjustments, 70. *See also* Skill and competency

Skills, concrete, 87, 94, 98

Skills, critical, 6, 25, 26, 29, 33, 77, 99, 164

Skills four-legged stool, 96, 97

Skills management: pay and rewards and paying for skill, 96-97

Skills library, 100; Internet and paying for skills, 98; paying for skill and competency on the Web, 82

Skills, paying for; and business value and the Internet, 10, 95-101; and competency on the Web, 82; conclusion, 100-101; four-legged stool, 96; innovation in, 96; and the Internet, 97-100; and pay and rewards, 96-97; problems the Web solves, 100

SMART objectives, 53

Software development company, 53

Southwest Airlines, 27, 163

Transparency, 8, 11; and incentive principles in contact center and distribution centers, 58-59; and SEC's proxy disclosure rules, 114

U

Unit of measurement, 59-60

United Airlines, 163

Unstable provider sample: selecting pay and rewards computer and Web-based products, 145

Upside opportunity, 115; meaningful 7, 43

U.S. Postal Service (USPS), 11, 12; organizational success at, 131-132

U.S. Postal Service (USPS), pay for performance: business case shows success, 140; communications and involvement, 138-139; concrete metrics, 134-135; leadership champions of, 134; meaningful reward differences, 135-137; success criteria for, 133-134; time to make the system work, 139; works, a powerful business case, 131-140

U.S. Senate Finance Committee, 121

V

Value added, 154; and business goal plan, 49; Economic Value Added (EVA) Variable Pay Program (USPS), 135, 139; sustained, 72, 73

Value of work, 69; and compensable elements, 79; measuring the, 9, 75-83. *See also* Job valuing

Valuing, base pay: predicting the future of total pay, 153, 154

Variable pay, 2, 3, 7, 8, 9, 24, 41, 73, 158; EVA Variable Pay Program (USPS), 135, 139; and incentives: double barreled solution to address pay for performance, 69-70; six principles of total rewards, 42-43

Variable pay and incentives: to support creating a performance culture, 70

Visible change: improving base pay for performance, 71

W

Wal-Mart, 162, 163

Web, the, 76, 80, 81, 82, 97; paying for skill and competency on, 82; problems solves on paying for skills, 100; and the USPS Pay For Performance Program, 138. *See also* Internet

Web products, 11; advantages of, 143-144; human resource pay and rewards: evaluating computer and, 13, 141-145; infrastructure and substance, 141-142; needs for the next decade, 142; next decade, 145; selecting products, 143-145; shortcomings of, 144-145

Web management of pay and rewards: innovation in paying for skills, 96

Web-based, 8, 10, 75, 96, 97, 141, 143; technologies, 82; the technology factor in job valuing, 81

Win-win, 1, 2, 5, 6, 7, 29, 30, 42, 44, 47, 65, 91, 135, 151, 152, 158, 159, 164; culture, 19

Win-win rewards: business performance culture branding, 31

Work supervised, type of: compensable elements, 80

Working Mother, 28, 29, 151, 160

Workplace brand: and business performance culture, 30-31; creating a powerful customized rewards, 6, 27-32; for your company, 31-32; unique, 27-28; who is branding, 28-29; why brand, 29-30

Workplace design, 29

WorldatWork, 20, 45

World-class sustained: setting stretch performance expectations, 52

WorldCom, 119

The Authors

Patricia K. Zingheim, Ph.D., and Jay R. Schuster, Ph.D.

Patricia K. Zingheim and Jay R. Schuster are partners in Schuster-Zingheim and Associates Inc., a pay and rewards consulting firm founded in 1985 in Los Angeles. They advise companies about aligning pay and total rewards with business strategy and consult on total rewards strategy, variable pay and incentives, base pay, performance management, executive compensation, sales compensation, team pay and recognition. They are co-authors of two best-selling pay books, *Pay People Right! Breakthrough Reward Strategies to Create Great Companies* (2000) and *The New Pay: Linking Employee and Organizational Performance* (1996), as well as more than 100 articles in business and professional journals and magazines. They are frequently quoted in publications such as *Fortune, Wall Street Journal, Across the Board, Working Woman* and *Harvard Management Update*.

Pat and Jay won WorldatWork's 2006 Keystone Award. They join 17 other recipients since 1995 in earning the highest honor WorldatWork gives for outstanding achievement in the field of compensation, benefits and total rewards. They were also selected as pay and motivation gurus in *The Guru Guide: The Best Ideas of the Top Management Thinkers*.

Recognized leaders in the move to new pay and experts on the role of pay in accelerating company growth and bottom-line performance, Pat and Jay speak throughout the world about how companies, people and rewards interact to add value to a business and how best to align total rewards with business goals. They have appeared on CNBC, CNN, NBC, CBS and other business talk shows. Pat earned her master of arts degree and Ph.D. from The Ohio State University and bachelor of arts degree from the University of Michigan. Jay earned his Ph.D. from the University of Southern California and his bachelor of arts and master of arts degrees from the University of Minnesota. Their Web site is www.paypeopleright.com.

The Co-authors

Marvin G. Dertien is co-author of Chapter 8, "Measuring the Value of Work." As research manager for ERI Economic Research Institute, Marv has overseen data collection, analyses and development of compensation data sets and geographical pay differences for more than 800 corporate clients during the past decade. His previous experience includes managing compensation and benefits for Pacific Telecom Inc., an international telecommunications company headquartered in Washington state. A pioneer in multiple regression studies, Marv served as a compensation manager of the Salt River Project, where he helped develop a market-based job classification system that was nondiscriminatory. Marv is trained in multiple programming code languages and has published articles in *Personnel Journal* and *Compensation & Benefits Review*. He is a member of WorldatWork and a past member of the American Public Power Compensation Committee. Marv earned his bachelor of science degree in economics from the University of Nebraska.

David J. Thomsen, Ph.D., ASA, CCP, is first author of Chapter 14, "Executive Compensation within Nonprofits: Rewarding Excellence and Ensuring Governance." He is the founder of ERI Economic Research Institute and a senior member of the American Society of Appraisers. Dave earned a CCP with WorldatWork and a Ph.D. in management analysis. He has served as a principal with William M. Mercer, senior vice president of American Stores, manager of compensation for Dart Industries, and managing director of Baker, Thomsen Associates (a West Coast benefits consulting firm). He currently leads ERI research efforts as they relate to Assessor Series software programs, the Geographic Reference Report® and ERI Web sites. He was the original author of both SHRM's first accreditation test in compensation and benefits and ACA's quantitative certification course and test. In addition, he authored hundreds of articles; the novel, *Merger, Takeover Conspiracy*; and ERI's quarterly *Update Newsletters*.

Paul Weatherhead is co-author of Chapter 15, "Pay for Performance Works: The U.S. Postal Service Presents a Powerful Business Case." He is pay program manager at the U.S. Postal Service. He works on the USPS Pay For Performance Program, which received the 2006 Excellence in Human Capital Management Award from The Performance Institute. He has been a contributor to major compensation changes during the past 15 years, such as the development of group incentive plans, executive and managerial merit pay programs, market-based salary structures and flexible spending accounts. Prior to his work at the USPS, he spent 13 years with Mobil Oil Corp. in a variety of human resources and labor relations positions. Paul earned a master's degree in labor and industrial relations from Michigan State University and an undergraduate degree from the University of Virginia, and has taught courses in human resource management, compensation and benefits and labor relations at the University of Virginia.